Occasions

Published by Kimblewick Publishing

Copyright © 2011 by David Rawlins

ISBN 978-0-9569965-0-3

Printed in the UK by
Hanley Print Services

OCCASIONS

A collection of thoughtful quotes & phrases:

Over 1,000 ways to say what you want to say.

Introduction

Everyone knows the excitement of giving and receiving cards. There seems to be a growing list of occasions when a card is sent; be it birthdays, weddings, christenings, anniversaries, Christmas greeting, valentines day or sadly death, divorce, ill-health or loss of some kind.

Recently I had to write on a birthday card for my mother, a wedding card for a friend and a maternity card for a work colleague. As usual I was rushing and ended up just putting "Best Wishes" and my name on all of them. Hardly inspiring and worse still it did not convey what I wanted to say at all. I had missed my opportunity.

I have opened hundreds of cards, but I can only remember those where the sender has put in that little extra effort to chose just the right words. Everybody I know has at some time faced the dilemma of what to write inside the card. Faced with the blank page we can so often find ourselves unable to conjure up the words. This book is here to help.

In the United Kingdom it is estimated that one billion pounds are spent on greeting cards every year, with the average person sending 55 cards annually. For such a great deal of expenditure, how often do we get our message, the message we want to convey, across effectively. When people receive cards they do look at the message; but how often are they delighted, intrigued or even surprised? The aim of this book is to make your message memorable.

Each quotation is included to help you with the hardest part of sending a card…what to say inside. Of course not everybody needs help all of the time, sometimes the words come along easily and fit just right, but if you are like me and are often stuck for something to say why struggle when you can learn from those who have gone before.

The best messages are those from the heart and I suggest when looking for something to say let your inner-self decide from those on offer.

Each chapter addresses a specific subject and contains messages from the obvious through to the cryptic (with some naughty ones along the way). Some of the phrases you may have seen before and wherever possible I have sought to name the author. Choose your selection carefully, remember who is going to read it try to picture their face as they read your message and decide if it will have the desired effect.

There are over a thousand quotes, a thousand ways to get your message across from Irish to Malayan proverbs, from William Shakespeare to Woody Allen

Please remember that these are quotations from other people so wherever possible, as I have done, always credit the author.

All quotations remain the intellectual property of their respective originations. I do not assert any claim of copyright for individual quotations. All use of quotations is done under the fair use copyright principle.

Whatever you want to say I hope you will find some inspiration in the following pages

David Rawlins

Contents

Anniversary

Grow old along with me, the best is yet to be. ~ BROWNING, Robert

Your love keeps on shining brightly
Throughout the trials of life
You're a wonderful example
Of a loving man and wife ~ Anonymous

A wedding anniversary is the celebration of love, trust,
partnership, tolerance and tenacity. The order varies for any
given year. ~ SWEENEY, Paul

Love does not consist of gazing at each other, but in looking
together in the same direction. ~ SAINT-EXUPERY, Antoine de

Spouse: someone who'll stand by you
through all the trouble you wouldn't have had
if you'd stayed single. ~ Anonymous

It's so great to find that one special person
You want to annoy for the rest of your life. ~ Anonymous

A successful marriage requires falling in love many times,
always with the same person. ~ MCLAUGHLIN, Mignon

May memories of all that you've shared
Be in your hearts today,
And may they fill the coming years
With love that's here to stay. ~ Anonymous

Anniversary

Remember, never go to bed mad. Stay up and fight. ~ Anonymous

You two have been singing
Right from the start
A secret song of loving care
Sung only from the heart ~ Anonymous

Remembering you both
When your special day is here
With all the warmth and feeling
That's felt for you all year ~ Anonymous

As you recall
your years together
remember that the best
is yet to come ~ Anonymous

A life without love is like a year without summer. ~ Swedish Proverb

A true lover always feels in debt to the one he loves. ~ SOCKMAN, Ralph W.

Chains do not hold a marriage together. It is threads, hundreds of tiny threads, which sew people together through the years. ~ SIGNORET, Simone

For it was not into my ear you whispered, but into my heart. It was not my lips you kissed, but my soul. ~ GARLAND, Judy

Anniversary

I don't pretend to know what love is for everyone, but I can tell you what it is for me; love is knowing all about someone, and still wanting to be with them more than any other person, love is trusting them enough to tell them everything about yourself, including the things you might be ashamed of, love is feeling comfortable and safe with someone, but still getting weak knees when they walk into a room and smile at you.

~ Anonymous

*I wouldn't change a thing
as happiness you bring.
You are my soul mate.
A marriage made by fate*

~ PULSIFER Catherine

If I know what love is, it is because of you.

~ HESSE, Herman

Life's greatest happiness is to be convinced we are loved.

~ HUGO, Victor

Love is just a word until someone comes along and gives it meaning.

~ PALAHNIUK, Chuck

Love is something eternal; the aspect may change, but not the essence.

~ GOGH, Vincent van

Love seems the swiftest, but it is the slowest of all growths. No man or woman really knows what perfect love is until they have been married a quarter of a century.

~ TWAIN, Mark

Married couples who love each other tell each other a thousand things without talking.

~ Chinese Proverb

Anniversary

Oh the comfort, the inexpressible comfort of feeling safe with a person, having neither to weigh thoughts nor measure words, but pouring them all right out, just as they are.

~ MULOCK, Dinah Maria

Our anniversary is a time to look back at the good times and a time to look ahead to live our dreams together.

~ PULSIFER, Catherine

Our wedding was many years ago. The celebration continues to this day.

~ PERRET, Gene

The best love is the kind that awakens the soul and makes us reach for more; that plants a fire in our hearts and brings peace to our minds.... That's what you've given me and that's what I hope to give to you forever.

~ The Notebook

The bonds of matrimony are like any other bonds - they mature slowly.

~ VRIES, Peter De

The most wonderful of all things in life, I believe, is the discovery of another human being with whom one's relationship has a growing depth, beauty, and joy as the years increase. This inner progressiveness of love between two human beings is a most marvellous thing; it cannot be found by looking for it or by passionately wishing for it. It is a sort of divine accident, and the most wonderful of all things in life.

~ WALPOLE, SR. Hugh

The secret to having a good marriage is to understand that marriage must be total, it must be permanent and it must be equal.

~ PITTMAN, Frank

Anniversary

There is no feeling more comforting and consoling than knowing   ~   Anonymous
you are right next to the one you love.

To love is to receive a glimpse of heaven.   ~   SUNDE, Karen

You can't stop loving or wanting to love because when its right,   ~   SWEAT, Keith
it's the best thing in the world. When you're in a relationship and
it's good, even if nothing else in your life is right, you feel like your
whole world is complete.

You don't marry someone you can live with - you marry the person   ~   Anonymous
who you cannot live without.

Still very active   ~   Anonymous
You're so rarely seen apart
You're just teenage geriatrics
So very young at heart

Wishing you all the very best,   ~   Anonymous
A great day a time for rest --
Good health, good luck, good friends,
And a happiness that never ends!

Love one another and you will be happy.   ~   LEUNIG, Michael
It's as simple and as difficult as that.

Remember, if you smoke after sex   ~   ALLEN, Woody
you're doing it too fast.

Anniversary

Love is not the dying moan of a distant violin
- it's the triumphant twang of a bedspring.

~ PERELMAN, S.J.

Take a generous dose of love
Add a measure or two of respect
Mix in some co-operation
Stir with the spoon of kindness
Add a dash of affection
A cuddle or two to taste
And a goodly dollop of humour
Sprinkle on tolerance and patience
Bake it in a bowl of friendship
And what have you got?
Your marriage through the years

~ Anonymous

Baby/Christening

"Babies are always more trouble than you thought - and more wonderful!" ~ OSGOOD, Charles

"A baby is God's way of saying the world should go on." ~ SMITH, Doris

"People who say they sleep like a baby usually don't have one!" ~ BURKE, Leo J.

"A baby's feet, like sea-shells pink Might tempt, should heaven sea meet, An angel's lips to kiss, we think, A baby's feet." ~ SWINBURNE, Algernon Charles

Bitter are the tears of a child: Sweeten them.
Deep are the thoughts of a child: Quiet them.
Sharp is the grief of a child: Take it from him.
Soft is the heart of a child: Do not harden it. ~ GLENCONNE, Pamela

To understand your parents' love, you must raise children yourself. ~ Chinese Proverb

"Every baby born into the world is a finer one than the last!" ~ DICKENS, Charles

There is no friendship, no love, like that of the parent for the child. ~ BEECHER, Henry Ward

"Did you ever notice that a new baby always seem to bear a striking resemblance to the relative who has the most money?" ~ PAUL, Robert

Making the decision to have a child is momentous. It is to decide forever to have your heart go walking around outside your body. ~ STONE, Elizabeth

Baby/Christening

"If evolution really works, how come mothers only have two hands?" ~ BERLE, Milton

" I always wondered why babies spend so much time sucking their thumbs. Then I tasted baby food!" ~ ORBEN, Robert

"Parenthood: The state of being better chaperoned than you were before marriage!" ~ COX, Marcelene

"Before I got married, I had six theories about bringing up children. Now, I have six children and no theories!" ~ WILMOT, John, Earl of Rochester

"You can learn many things from children. How much patience you have, for instance!" ~ JONES, Franklin P.

"Raising kids is part joy and part guerilla warfare!" ~ ASNER, Ed

"If your baby's beautiful and perfect, never cries or fusses, sleeps on schedule and burps on demand, an angel all the time, you're the grandma!" ~ BLOOMINGDALE, Theresa

"Families with babies and families without babies are sorry for each other!" ~ HOWE, Ed

"It sometimes happens, even in the best of families, that a baby is born. This is not necessarily cause for alarm. The important thing is to keep your wits about you and borrow some money!" ~ SMITH, Elinor Goulding

Baby/Christening

"The worst feature of a new baby is its mother's singing!" ~ HUBBARD, Ken

Most mothers are instinctive philosophers. ~ STOWE, Harriet Beecher

Nothing else will ever make you as happy or as sad, as proud or as tired, as motherhood. ~ PARSONS, Elia

"Babies are such a nice way to start people!" ~ HERROLD, Don

"A baby is born with a need to be loved - and never outgrows it!" ~ CLARK, Frank A.

"I didn't think that having a baby after I'd turned forty was so bad - only that I had to hold her at arm's length to look at her!" ~ HAYNES, Margie

"A woman can learn a lot from holding a new baby. It is life beginning again - sweet possibilities! No problem in the world is big enough to be remembered." ~ MCOMBER, Susan

"A baby is an angel whose wings decrease as his legs increase!" ~ TWAIN, Mark

"Always kiss your children goodnight - even if they're already asleep!" ~ BROWN, JR H. Jackson

"There are three reasons for breast-feeding: the milk is always at the right temperature; it comes in attractive containers and the cat can't get it!" ~ CHALMERS, Irena

11

Baby/Christening

"I realize why women die in childbirth - it's preferable!"   ~   GLASER, Sherry

"If nature had arranged that husbands and wives should have children alternatively, there would never be more than three in a family!"   ~   HOUSMAN, Lawrence

For the mother is and must be, whether she knows it or not, the greatest, strongest and most lasting teacher her children have.   ~   SMITH, Hannah W.

There is a religion in all deep love, but the love of a mother is the veil of a softer light between the heart and the heavenly Father.   ~   COLERIDGE, Samuel Taylor

"Parents love their children, more than children love their parents"   ~   Auctoritates Aristotelis

Men love their wives, women love their children, and children love their hamsters.   ~   Anonymous

You should never have children, only grandchildren   ~   Anonymous

A Baby is a Blessing
Truly from Heaven above
A Precious, Sweet Angel
To Cherish and to Love.   ~   Anonymous

Children are love made visible.   ~   Anonymous

May your lovely little daughter /son
So very precious and new   ~   Anonymous

Baby/Christening

Bring a life full of pleasure
And happiness all to you

Mummy, I thought you were   ~ Anonymous
Just getting fat,
But we've got a baby
HOW COOL IS THAT!

You came into my life   ~ Anonymous
Expected, but still a surprise
There were centuries of wisdom
Looking out from your big (blue) eyes
I held you so tightly in my arms
Traced your fingers that were gently curled
Through tears of joy, I whispered quietly
My beautiful grandchild

A special little Baby Girl   ~ Anonymous
May sunshine fill her days
May rainbows light her path in life
And angels full sing her praise

A crying baby is the best form of birth control.   ~ TABRON, Carole

A baby is a blank cheque made payable to the human race.   ~ SEIFERT, Barbara Christine

Having a child is surely the most beautifully irrational act that two people in love can commit.   ~ COSBY, Bill

Every child begins the world again.   ~ THOREAU, Henry David

Baby/Christening

Adam and Eve had many advantages, but the principal one was that they escaped teething.   ~ TWAIN, Mark

The moment a child is born, the mother is also born. She never existed before. The woman existed, but the mother, never. A mother is something absolutely new.   ~ Rajneesh

The angels danced on the day your baby was born. Babies are bundles from Heaven   ~ Anonymous

Bereavement/Sympathy

"Weep not for the fallen,
But thank God that they lived"   ~ Anonymous

May the peace which comes from the memories of love shared,   ~ Anonymous
comfort you now and in the days ahead.

Death is not a full stop, but a comma in the story of life   ~ Anonymous

To die must be a really big adventure   ~ BARRIE, J.M.

If you walk towards the sun, the shadows fall away   ~ Anonymous

Your joy is your sorrow unmasked...   ~ GIBRAN, Kahlil
When you are joyous, look deep into your heart and you shall find
it is only that which has given you sorrow that is giving you joy.
When you are sorrowful, look again in your heart, and you shall
see that in truth you are weeping for that which has been your
delight.

He who has a why to live for can survive any how   ~ Nietzsche

Death is nothing at all – I have only slipped away into the next   ~ HOLLAND, Canon
room. I am I and you are you. Whatever we were to each other,   Scott
that we still are.

Sorrow is not for ever, love is   ~ Anonymous

Sorrow, like a river, must be given vent, lest it erode the bank   ~ Mexican proverb

Bereavement/Sympathy

I am learning to look at your life again
Instead of your death and departing

~ PIZER, Marjorie

Sorrow that has no vent in tears makes other organs weep

~ Anonymous

"Now I lay me down to sleep,
I pray the Lord my soul to keep,
If I should die before I wake,
I pray the Lord my soul to take "

~ Anonymous

"Abide with me: fast falls the eventide;
The darkness deepens; Lord with me abide:
When other helpers fail, and comforts flee,
Help of the helpless, O abide with me."

~ LYTE, Henry Francis

"Do not stand at my grave and weep,
I am not there,
I do not sleep,
I am a thousand winds that blow,
I am the diamond glints on snow,
I am the sunlight on ripened grain,
I am the gentle autumn rain,
When you awaken in the morning's rush,
I am the swift uplifting rush of quiet birds,
In circled flight,
I am the soft stars that shine at night,
Do not stand at my grave and cry,
I am not there,
I did not die"

~ Anonymous

Bereavement/Sympathy

The bitterest tears shed over graves are for words left unsaid and for deeds left undone.

~ STOWE, Harriet Beecher

Believe that life is worth living, and your belief will help create the fact

~ Anonymous

Perhaps they are not the stars, but rather openings in heaven where the love of our lost ones pours through and shines down upon us to let us know they are happy.

~ Anonymous

In the night of death, hope sees a star, and listening love can hear the rustle of a wing.

~ Anonymous

Those whom the heart of man shuts out, Sometimes the heart of God takes in, And fences them all round about, With silence 'mid the world's loud din.

~ Anonymous

He who has gone, so we but cherish his memory, abides with us, more potent, nay, more present than the living man.

~ Anonymous

What moves through us is a silence, a quiet sadness, a longing for one more day, one more word, one more touch, we may not understand why you left this earth so soon, or why you left before we were ready to say good-bye, but little by little, we begin to remember not just that you died, but that you lived. And that your life gave us memories too beautiful to forget.

~ Anonymous

God saw you getting tired and a cure was not to be. So He put His arms around you and whispered "come to me." With tearful eyes we watched you, and saw you pass away. Although we loved you

~ Anonymous

Bereavement/Sympathy

dearly, we could not make you stay. A golden heart stopped beating, hardworking hands at rest. God broke our hearts to prove to us, He only takes the best.

Birthday

Happy Birthday and remember: We don't stop playing because we grow old; we grow old because we stop playing. ~ Anonymous

"The secret of staying young is to live honestly, eat slowly, and lie about your age!" ~ BALL, Lucille

"Cheer up! The worst is yet to come!" ~ JOHNSON, Philander Chase.

I bet if you had known you would live so long, you would have taken better care of yourself. ~ Anonymous

"Middle age is when your age starts to show around your middle!" ~ HOPE, Bob

"A diplomat is a man who always remembers a woman's birthday but never remembers her age!" ~ FROST, Robert

"Birthdays are good for you. Statistics show that the people who have the most live the longest !" ~ LORENZONI, Larry

"Age is strictly a case of mind over matter. If you don't mind, it doesn't matter !" ~ BENNY, Jack

"The old believe everything; the middle-aged suspect everything; the young know everything!" ~ WILDE, Oscar

"Old age is like everything else. To make a success of it, you've got to start young!" ~ ASTAIRE, Fred

Birthday

"It takes a long time to grow young !" ~ PICASSO, Pablo

"Youth comes but once in a lifetime!" ~ LONGFELLOW, Henry Wadsworth

"The years between fifty and seventy are the hardest. You are always being asked to do things, and yet you are not decrepit enough to turn them down!" ~ ELIOT T. S.

"We are always the same age inside" ~ STEIN, Gertrude

"Forty is the old age of youth; fifty is the youth of old age!" ~ Anonymous

"At twenty years of age, the will reigns; at thirty, the wit; and at forty, the judgement." ~ FRANKLIN, Benjamin

"You take all the experience and judgement of men over fifty out of the world and there wouldn't be enough left to run it!" ~ FORD, Henry

Today, be aware of how you are spending your beautiful moments, and spend them wisely. ~ Anonymous

Happy Birthday. My thoughts are always free to go anywhere, but it's surprising how often they head in your direction. ~ Anonymous

When we're together or when we're apart, you're first in my thoughts and first in my heart. Have a lovely birthday ~ Anonymous

Birthday

May the bird of paradise fly up your nose. May an elephant caress you with his toes
You can not prevent the birds of sorrow from flying over your head, but you can prevent them from building a nest in your hair .

~ Chinese Proverb

Happy Birthday
How did it get so late so soon?
It's night before it's afternoon.
December is here before its June.
My goodness how the time has flown.
How did it get so late so soon?

~ SEUSS, Dr.

As you slide down the banister of life, may all the splinters point in the right direction.

~ Anonymous

Remember: Life is like a bowl of peppers, what you do today, may burn your arse tomorrow.

~ Anonymous

Sorry my card didn't quite make it on time. If only you were born a couple of days later – we might have avoided this whole ugly incident!.

~ Anonymous

The days go buy so quickly and it is suddenly your Birthday again so soon. I hope this gets to you in time, but if not sorry for being a little late. Many happy returns.

~ Anonymous

No woman is ever old enough to know better.

~ Anonymous

The secret of longevity is to keep breathing

~ Anonymous

Birthday

From here on in start each day by reading the obituaries, if you're not in them, get up ~ Anonymous

"Middle age is when you are sitting at home on a Saturday night and the telephone rings and you hope it isn't for you" ~ NASH, Ogden

"This birthday greeting is intended only for the use of the addressee and may contain confidential or legally privileged information. The greeting extended by the author is not a greeting from the Department unless explicitly stated as such by an officer with an appropriate security clearance or delegation..." ~ Anonymous

"...it's not working, and I can't live like this anymore. I don't care who knows about us, and I can't believe you're going to stand there stuffing your face with cake and laughing with everybody like nothing happened after the way you treated me last night..." ~ Anonymous

Inside every older person is a younger person - wondering what the hell happened. ~ ARMSTRONG, Cora Harvey

There is still no cure for the common birthday. ~ GLENN, John

To me, old age is always 15 years older than I am. ~ BARUCH, Bernard

Old age isn't so bad when you consider the alternative. ~ CHEVALIER, Maurice

I'm at an age when my back goes out more than I do. ~ DILLER, Phyllis

Birthday

You are only young once, but you can be immature for a lifetime.   ~   GRIER, John P.

Let us respect grey hairs, especially our own.   ~   SEARS, J. P.

Age is a high price to pay for maturity.   ~   STOPPARD, Tom

Growing old is like being increasingly penalized
for a crime you have not committed.   ~   POWELL, Anthony

Birthdays are nature's way of telling us to eat more cake.   ~   Anonymous

There is still no cure for the common birthday.   ~   GLENN John

May you live all the days of your life.   ~   SWIFT, Jonathan

Let us celebrate the occasion with wine and sweet words.   ~   Plautus

Age is not measured by years. Nature does not equally distribute
energy. Some people are born old and tired while others are
going strong at seventy.   ~   THOMPSON, Dorothy

And in the end, it's not the years in your life that count. It's the life
in your years.   ~   LINCOLN, Abraham

At middle age the soul should be opening up like a rose, not
closing up like a cabbage.   ~   HOLMES, John Andrew

Birthday

Few women admit their age. Few men act theirs. ~ Anonymous

From birth to age eighteen, a girl needs good parents. From eighteen to thirty-five, she needs good looks. From thirty-five to fifty-five, she needs a good personality. From fifty-five on, she needs good cash. ~ TUCKER, Sophie

It is better to wear out than to rust out. ~ CUMBERLAND, Bishop Richard

Life begins at forty. ~ PITKIN, W. B.

Middle age is when you've met so many people that every new person you meet reminds you of someone else. ~ NASH, Ogden

Nature gives you the face you have at twenty, but it's up to you to merit the face you have at fifty. ~ CHANEL, Coco

Once I was looking through the kitchen window at dusk and I saw an old woman looking in. Suddenly the light changed and I realized that the old woman was myself. You see, it all happens on the outside; inside one doesn't change. ~ KEANE, Molly

Sing a song of Birthdays
Full of fun and cheer
And may you keep on having them
For many a happy year. ~ Anonymous

Some people, no matter how old they get, never lose their beauty - they merely move it from their faces into their hearts. ~ BUXBAUM, Martin

Birthday

The advantage of being eighty years old is that one has many people to love.   ~ RENOIR, Jean

The Best way to remember your wife's birthday is to forget it once.   ~ PROCHNOW, H. V.

The lovely thing about being forty is that you can appreciate twenty-five-year-old men.   ~ MC CULLOUGH, Colleen

Middle age is when work is a lot less fun and fun is a lot more work.   ~ Anonymous

The more you praise and celebrate your life, the more there is in life to celebrate.   ~ WINFREY, Oprah

The older the fiddler, the sweeter the tune.   ~ English Proverb

What could be more beautiful than a dear old lady growing wise with age? Every age can be enchanting, provided you live within it.   ~ BARDOT, Brigitte

Whatever with the past has gone, The best is always yet to come.   ~ LARCOM, Lucy

When you turn thirty, a whole new thing happens: you see yourself acting like you parents.   ~ SABOL, Blair

You grow up the day you have your first real laugh at yourself.   ~ BARRYMORE, Ethel

Birthday

Youth is happy because it has the ability to see beauty. Anyone who keeps the ability to see beauty never grows old.   ~ KAFKA, Franz

There are three hundred and sixty-four days when you might get un-birthday presents ... and only one for birthday presents, you know.   ~ CARROLL, Lewis

No wise man ever wished to be younger.   ~ SWIFT, Jonathan

One of the signs of passing youth is the birth of a sense of fellowship with other human beings as we take our place among them.   ~ WOOLF, Virginia

Grow old along with me!
The best is yet to be...   ~ BROWNING, Robert

We know we're getting old when the only thing we want for our birthday is not to be reminded of it.   ~ Anonymous

Believing hear, what you deserve to hear:
Your birthday as my own to me is dear...
But yours gives most; for mine did only lend
Me to the world; yours gave to me a friend.   ~ MARTIAL, Marcus Valerius

Because time itself is like a spiral, something special happens on your birthday each year: The same energy that God invested in you at birth is present once again.   ~ SCHNEERSON, Menachem Mendel

Growing old is mandatory; growing up is optional.   ~ DAVIS, Chili

Birthday

They say that age is all in your mind. The trick is keeping it from creeping down into your body.   ~ Anonymous

Time may be a great healer, but it's a lousy beautician.   ~ Anonymous

May flowers always line your path and sunshine light your day.
May songbirds serenade you every step along the way.
May a rainbow run beside you in a sky that's always blue.
And may happiness fill your heart each day your whole life through.   ~ Irish Blessing

Sing a song of Birthdays Full of fun and cheer And may you keep on having them For many a happy year.   ~ Anonymous

Middle Age: When you begin to exchange your emotions for symptoms.   ~ CLEMENCEAU, Georges

Middle age is the awkward period when
Father Time catches up with Mother Nature.   ~ COFFIN, Harold

Middle age is having a choice between two temptations and choosing the one that'll get you home earlier.   ~ BENNETT, Dan

Middle age is the time when a man is always thinking that in a week or two he will feel as good as ever.   ~ MARQUIS, Don

Thirty-five is when you finally get your head together and your body starts falling apart.   ~ LESCHEN, Caryn

Birthday

After 30, a body has a mind of its own. — MIDLER, Bette

Thirty five is a very attractive age;
London society is full of women who have of their own
free choice remained thirty-five for years — WILDE, Oscar

What most persons consider as virtue,
after the age of 40 is simply a loss of energy. — Voltaire

The first forty years of life give us the text: the next thirty supply
the commentary. — SCHOPENHAUER, Arthur

Every man over forty is a scoundrel. — SHAW, George Bernard

Life begins at 40 - but so do fallen arches, rheumatism, faulty
eyesight, and the tendency to tell a story to the same person,
three or four times. — ROWLAND, Helen

At the age of 20, we don't care what the world thinks of us; at 30,
we worry about what it is thinking of us; at 40, we discover that it
wasn't thinking of us at all. — Anonymous

Forty isn't old.................if you're a tree — Anonymous

The "I just woke up" face of your 30's is the "all day long" face of
your 40's — REID, Libby

You're not 40, you're eighteen with 22 years experience. — Anonymous

Birthday

The best years of a woman's life - the ten years between 39 and 40   ~   Anonymous

Looking fifty is great--if you're sixty.   ~   RIVERS, Joan

At age 50, everyone has the face he deserves.   ~   ORWELL, George

"Forget about the past, you can't change it.
Forget about the future, you can't predict it.
Forget about the present, I didn't get you one."   ~   Anonymous

"I intend to live forever - so far, so good!"   ~   WRIGHT, Stephen

"Age is strictly a case of mind over matter. If you don't mind, it doesn't matter."   ~   BENNY, Jack

"You know you are getting old when the candles cost more than the cake."   ~   HOPE, Bob

All my life, I always wanted to be somebody. Now I see that I should have been more specific."   ~   WAGNER, Jane

"Happiness is good health and a bad memory."   ~   BERGMAN, Ingrid

"Wrinkles should merely indicate where smiles have been."   ~   TWAIN, Mark

"If you want to look young and thin, hang around old fat people."   ~   EASON, Jim

Birthday

"Be kind to your kids, they'll be choosing your nursing home." ~ Anonymous

"First you forget names; then you forget faces; then you forget to zip up your fly; and then you forget to unzip your fly." ~ RICKEY, Branch Rickey

"Wisdom doesn't necessarily come with age. Sometimes age just shows up all by itself." ~ WILSON, Tom

"Age is a number and mine is unlisted." ~ Anonymous

"A well-adjusted woman is one who not only knows what she wants for her birthday, but even knows what she's going to exchange it for." ~ Anonymous

"As you get older three things happen. The first is your memory goes, and I can't remember the other two." ~ Anonymous

"When I have a birthday I take the day off. But when my wife has a birthday, she takes a year or two off." ~ Anonymous

"To me, fair friend, you never can be old, For as you were when first your eye I eye'd, Such seems your beauty still." ~ SHAKESPEARE, William

"Middle age is when you still believe you'll feel better in the morning!" ~ HOPE, Bob

"Live as long as you may, the first twenty years are the longest half of your life!" ~ SOUTHEY, Robert

Birthday

The really frightening thing about middle age is that you know   ~   DAY, Doris
you'll grow out of it!"

The prime of life depends on the age of the person doing the   ~   Anonymous
talking

The time of your life has become a struggle to keep your weight   ~   Anonymous
down and your spirits up

You can live this life but once, but if you live it right, once is   ~   Anonymous
enough

Happy Birthday and remember: ~   Anonymous
Be yourself
Always be true
Stand up for yourself
Take one day at a time
Allow time for yourself
Relax
Do unto others as they would do to you
Do unto others as they would do to you
Insist on your rights
Champion yourself
Keep the faith
Hold yourself responsible
Each day is a gift
Allow yourself to enjoy yourself
Don't take life too seriously

Christmas

What is Christmas? It is tenderness for the past, courage for the present, hope for the future. It is a fervent wish that every cup may overflow with blessings rich and eternal, and that every path may lead to peace.

~ PHARO, Agnes M.

Christmas is forever, not for just one day, for loving, sharing, giving, are not to put away like bells and lights and tinsel, in some box upon a shelf. The good you do for others is good you do yourself.

~ BROOKS, Norman W.

Whatever else be lost among the years,
Let us keep Christmas still a shining thing:
Whatever doubts assail us, or what fears,
Let us hold close one day, remembering
Its poignant meaning for the hearts of men.
Let us get back our childlike faith again.

~ CROWELL, Grace Noll

The wish is old,
The wish is true,
A merry Christmas,
My friends, to you

~ Anonymous

It is Christmas in the heart that puts Christmas in the air.

~ ELLIS, W.T.

It means so much
To keep in touch
...with special friends like you

~ Anonymous

Christmas

And the Grinch, stood puzzling and puzzling, how could it be so? ~ SEUSS, Dr.
It came without ribbons. It came without tags. It came without
packages, boxes or bags. And he puzzled and puzzled 'till his
puzzler was sore. Then the Grinch thought of something he
hadn't before. What if Christmas, he thought, doesn't come from a
store. What if Christmas, perhaps, means a little bit more.

Christmas, children, is not a date. It is a state of mind. ~ CHASE, Mary Ellen

Christmas Eve was a night of song that wrapped itself about you ~ ALDRICH, Bess
like a shawl. But it warmed more than your body. It warmed your Streeter
heart... filled it, too, with a melody that would last forever.

Christmas is the gentlest, loveliest festival of the revolving year - ~ CAMERON, W.J.
and yet, for all that, when it speaks, its voice has strong authority.

Christmas is most truly Christmas when we celebrate it by giving ~ STAPLETON, Ruth
the light of love to those who need it most. Carter

A hug is the perfect Christmas gift, one size fits all and it's easily ~ Anonymous
returned.

May your Christmas ~ Anonymous
be wrapped in Joy
and filled with Love
Best Wishes for
Peace, Health
and Happiness
throughout the coming year.

Christmas

After the gifts have all been opened
And the tree starts to wane
When the carols have long faded
May happiness remain

~ Anonymous

Wishing you
An everlasting Season
Of Peace and Goodwill

~ Anonymous

Here's to a stress free Christmas
May your tinsel be untangled and your Christmas lights work first time

~ Anonymous

This Christmas may you join, the angels rejoicing, the shepherds in believing, the wise men in seeking and the lads down the pub

~ Anonymous

I heard the bells on Christmas Day
Their old, familiar carols play,
And wild and sweet
The words repeat
Of peace on earth, good-will to men!

~ LONGFELLOW, Henry Wadsworth

Happy, happy Christmas, that can win us back to the delusions of our childish days; that can recall to the old man the pleasures of his youth; that can transport the sailor and the traveller, thousands of miles away, back to his own fireside and his quiet home!

~ DICKENS, Charles

Our hearts grow tender with childhood memories and love of kindred, and we are better throughout the year for having, in spirit, become a child again at Christmas-time.

~ WILDER, Laura Ingalls

Christmas

I will honour Christmas in my heart, and try to keep it all the year. ~ DICKENS, Charles

Christmas waves a magic wand over this world, and behold, everything is softer and more beautiful. ~ PEALE, Norman Vincent

Great little One! whose all-embracing birth
Lifts Earth to Heaven, stoops Heaven to Earth. ~ CRASHAW, Richard

At Christmas play and make good cheer,
For Christmas comes but once a year ~ TUSSER, Thomas

It is Christmas in the heart that puts Christmas in the air. ~ ELLIS, W.T.

He who has not Christmas in his heart will never find it under a tree. ~ SMITH, Roy L.

There has been only one Christmas - the rest are anniversaries. ~ CAMERON, W.J.

Christmas is the season for kindling the fire of hospitality in the hall, the genial flame of charity in the heart. ~ Washington Irving

One of the most glorious messes in the world is the mess created in the living room on Christmas day. Don't clean it up too quickly." ~ ROONEY, Andy

Love is what's in the room with you at Christmas if you stop opening presents and listen. ~ Anonymous

Christmas

Roses are reddish
Violets are bluish
If it weren't for Christmas
We'd all be Jewish.

~ HILL, Benny

Santa is very jolly because he knows where all the bad girls live.

~ MILLER, Dennis

Christmas began in the heart of God. It is complete only when it reaches the heart of man.

~ Anonymous

Blessed is the season which engages the whole world in a conspiracy of love.

~ MABI, Hamilton Wright

With Christmas you can forget the past with a present.

~ Anonymous

If there is no joyous way to give a festive gift, give love away.

~ Anonymous

Time was with most of us, when Christmas Day, encircling all our limited world like a magic ring, left nothing out for us to miss or seek; bound together all our home enjoyments, affections, and hopes; grouped everything and everyone round the Christmas fire, and make the little picture shining in our bright young eyes, complete.

~ DICKENS, Charles

Heap on the wood!-the wind is chill; But let it whistle as it will, We'll keep our Christmas merry still.

~ SCOTT, Sir Walter

"The earth has grown old with its burden of care But at Christmas it always is young, The heart of the jewel burns lustrous and fair

~ BROOKS, Phillips

Christmas

And its soul full of music breaks the air, When the song of angels is sung."

"It is Christmas in the heart that puts Christmas in the air." ~ ELLIS, W. T.

"The best of all gifts around any Christmas tree: the presence of a happy family all wrapped up in each other." ~ HILLIS, Burton

"Love came down at Christmas; Love all lovely, love divine; Love was born at Christmas, Stars and angels gave the sign." ~ ROSSETTI, Christina

"I am not alone at all, I thought. I was never alone at all. And that, of course, is the message of Christmas. We are never alone. Not when the night is darkest, the wind coldest, the word seemingly most indifferent. For this is still the time God chooses." ~ CALDWELL, Taylor

"What is Christmas? It is tenderness for the past, courage for the present, hope for the future. It is a fervent wish that every cup may overflow with blessings rich and eternal, and that every path may lead to peace." ~ PHARO, Agnes M.

"Bless us Lord, this Christmas, with quietness of mind; Teach us to be patient and always to be kind." ~ RICE, Helen Steiner

At Christmas play and make good cheer, For Christmas comes but once a year." ~ TUSSER, Thomas

"May Peace be your gift at Christmas and your blessing all year through!" ~ Anonymous

Christmas

"Where charity stands watching and faith holds wide the door the dark night wakes - the glory breaks, Christmas comes once more." ~ BROOKS, Phillips

"I heard the bells on Christmas Day. Their old familiar carols play. And wild and sweet the words repeat. Of peace on earth goodwill to men." ~ LONGFELLOW, Henry Wadsworth

"Like snowflakes, my Christmas memories gather and dance - each beautiful, unique and too soon gone." ~ WHIPP, Deborah

Christmas Day is a day of joy and charity. May God make you very rich in both. ~ BROOKS, Phillips

Blessed is the season which engages the whole world in a conspiracy of love! ~ MABIE, Hamilton Wright

Christmas begins about the first of December with an office party and ends when you finally realize what you spent, around April fifteenth of the next year. ~ O'ROURKE, P.J.

Christmas is a time when you get homesick - even when you're home. ~ NELSON, Carol

Christmas is the season when you buy this year's gifts with next year's money. ~ Anonymous

Anyone who believes that men are the equal of women has never seen a man trying to wrap a Christmas present. ~ Anonymous

Christmas

For the spirit of Christmas fulfils the greatest hunger of mankind. ~ SCHULER, Loring A.

I do like Christmas on the whole.... In its clumsy way, it does approach Peace and Goodwill. But it is clumsier every year. ~ FORSTER, E.M.

I have always thought of Christmas time, when it has come round, as a good time; a kind, forgiving, charitable time; the only time I know of, in the long calendar of the year, when men and women seem by one consent to open their shut-up hearts freely, and to think of people below them as if they really were fellow passengers ~ DICKENS, Charles

I love the Christmas-tide, and yet,
I notice this, each year I live;
I always like the gifts I get,
But how I love the gifts I give! ~ WELLS, Carolyn

I will honour Christmas in my heart, and try to keep it all the year. ~ DICKENS, Charles

I wish we could put up some of the Christmas spirit in jars and open a jar of it every month. ~ MILLER, Harlan

It comes every year and will go on forever. And along with Christmas belong the keepsakes and the customs. Those humble, everyday things a mother clings to, and ponders, like Mary in the secret spaces of her heart. ~ HOLMES, Marjorie

It is Christmas in the heart that puts Christmas in the air. ~ ELLIS, W.T.

Christmas

It is the one season of the year when we can lay aside all gnawing worry, indulge in sentiment without censure, assume the carefree faith of childhood, and just plain "have fun." Whether they call it Yuletide, Noel, Weinachten, or Christmas, people around the earth thirst for its refreshment as the desert traveller for the oasis.

~ MONROE, D.D.

It was always said of him, that he knew how to keep Christmas well, if any man alive possessed the knowledge. May that be truly said of us, and all of us! And so, as Tiny Tim observed, "God Bless Us, Every One!

~ DICKENS, Charles

Let the spirit of love gently fill our hearts and homes. In this loveliest of seasons may you find many reasons for happiness.

~ Anonymous

Never worry about the size of your Christmas tree. In the eyes of children, they are all 30 feet tall.

~ WILDE, Larry

Next to a circus there ain't nothing that packs up and tears out faster than the Christmas spirit.

~ HUBBARD, Kin

Nothing's as mean as giving a little child something useful for Christmas.

~ HUBBARD, Kin

Oh! lovely voices of the sky
Which hymned the Saviour's birth,
Are ye not singing still on high,
Ye that sang, "Peace on earth"?

~ HEMANS, Felicia

Christmas

Oh, for the good old days when people would stop Christmas shopping when they ran out of money.   ~ Anonymous

Once again we find ourselves enmeshed in the Holiday Season, that very special time of year when we join with our loved ones in sharing centuries-old traditions such as trying to find a parking space.   ~ BARRY, Dave

Peace on earth will come to stay, When we live Christmas every day.   ~ RICE, Helen Steiner

Perhaps the best Yuletide decoration is being wreathed in smiles.   ~ Anonymous

Remember, This December, That love weighs more than gold!   ~ BACON, Josephine Dodge Daskam

Sing hey! Sing hey! For Christmas Day; Twine mistletoe and holly. For a friendship glows In winter snows, And so let's all be jolly!   ~ Anonymous

Somehow, not only for Christmas,
But all the long year through,
The joy that you give to others,
Is the joy that comes back to you.
And the more you spend in blessing,
The poor and lonely and sad,
The more of your heart's possessing,
Returns to you glad.   ~ WHITTIER, John Greenleaf

What do you call people who are afraid of Santa Claus — Claustrophobic.   ~ Anonymous

Christmas

The earth has grown old with its burden of care, but at Christmas it always is young.   ~ BROOKS, Phillips

The Supreme Court has ruled that they cannot have a nativity scene in Washington, D.C. This wasn't for any religious reasons. They couldn't find three wise men and a virgin.   ~ LENO, Jay

There is a remarkable breakdown of taste and intelligence at Christmastime. Mature, responsible grown men wear neckties made of holly leaves and drink alcoholic beverages with raw egg yolks and cottage cheese in them.   ~ O'ROURKE, P.J.

What is Christmas? It is tenderness for the past, courage for the present, hope for the future. It is a fervent wish that every cup may overflow with blessings rich and eternal, and that every path may lead to peace.   ~ PHARO, Agnes M.

Whatever else be lost among the years, Let us keep Christmas still a shining thing: Whatever doubts assail us, or what fears, Let us hold close one day, remembering Its poignant meaning for the hearts of men. Let us get back our childlike faith again.   ~ CROWELL, Grace Noll

Wouldn't life be worth the living
Wouldn't dreams be coming true
If we kept the Christmas spirit
All the whole year through?   ~ Anonymous

Christmas, my child, is love in action. Every time we love, every time we give, it's Christmas.   ~ ROGERS, Dale Evans

Christmas

Christmas - that magic blanket that wraps itself about us, that something so intangible that it is like a fragrance. It may weave a spell of nostalgia. Christmas may be a day of feasting, or of prayer, but always it will be a day of remembrance - a day in which we think of everything we have ever loved.

~ RUNDEL,
Augusta E.

Congratulations

Congrats on passing your driving test
Remember don't drive faster
than your Guardian Angel can fly!

~ Anonymous

All successful people men and women are big dreamers. They imagine what their future could be, ideal in every respect, and then they work every day toward their distant vision, that goal or purpose.

~ TRACY, Brian

All our dreams can come true...if we have the courage to pursue them.

~ Walt Disney

An investment in knowledge always pays the best interest.

~ FRANKLIN, Benjamin

Don't judge each day by the harvest you reap but by the seeds that you plant.

~ STEVENSON, Robert Louis

Don't live down to expectations. Go out there and do something remarkable.

~ WASSERSTEIN, Wendy

Graduation is only a concept. In real life every day you graduate. Graduation is a process that goes on until the last day of your life. If you can grasp that, you'll make a difference.

~ PENCOVICI, Arie

Go confidently in the direction of your dreams. Live the life you have imagined.

~ THOREAU, Henry David

Go for it now. The future is promised to no one.

~ DYER, Wayne

Congratulations

Hitch your wagon to a star.
~ EMERSON, Ralph Waldo

I hope your dreams take you to the corners of your smiles, to the highest of your hopes, to the windows of your opportunities, and to the most special places your heart has ever known.
~ Anonymous

If you can imagine it, you can achieve it; if you can dream it, you can become it.
~ WARD, William Arthur

It takes courage to grow up and become who you really are.
~ CUMMINGS, E.E.

Just about a month from now I'm set adrift, with a diploma for a sail and lots of nerve for oars.
~ HALLIBURTON, Richard

My father always told me, "Find a job you love and you'll never have to work a day in your life."
~ FOX, Jim

Put your future in good hands - your own.
~ Anonymous

The fireworks begin today. Each diploma is a lighted match. Each one of you is a fuse.
~ KOCH, Edward

The future lies before you
Like a field of driven snow,
Be careful how you tread it,
For every step will show.
~ Author Unknown

Congratulations

The horizon leans forward, offering you space to place new steps of change. ~ ANGELOU, Maya

Things turn out best for the people who make the best out of the way things turn out. ~ Art Linkletter

Think big thoughts but relish small pleasures. ~ BROWN, H. Jackson

To accomplish great things, we must not only act, but also dream; not only plan, but also believe. ~ Anatole France

We cannot direct the wind but we can adjust the sails. ~ Anonymous

When you leave your college, don't forget why you went. ~ Anonymous

Wherever you go, go with all your heart. ~ Confucius

Wherever you go, no matter what the weather, always bring your own sunshine. ~ D'ANGELO, Anthony J.

Your schooling may be over, but remember that your education still continues. ~ Anonymous

I do not know beneath what sky
Nor on what seas shall be thy fate;
I only know it shall be high,
I only know it shall be great. ~ Anonymous

Congratulations

You have brains in your head.
You have feet in your shoes.
You can steer yourself
Any direction you choose.

~ SEUSS, Dr.

It's really great to know you've passed!
Now you can ditch those L-plates at last!
We know not where we're going, because the fates they will
decide, all we can but do is make damn sure we always enjoy the
ride.

~ Anonymous

Reach high, for stars lie hidden in your soul.
Dream deep, for every dream precedes the goal.

~ Anonymous

Divorce

The happiest time of anyone's life is just after the first divorce. ~ GALBRAITH, J. K.

Divorce is the psychological equivalent of a triple coronary bypass ~ BLAKELEY, Mary K

A divorce is like an amputation; you survive, but there's less of you. ~ ATWOOD, Margaret

Ah yes, divorce...from the Latin word meaning to rip out a man's genitals through his wallet ~ WILLIAMS, Robin

The only time my wife and I had a simultaneous orgasm was when the judge signed the divorce papers. ~ ALLEN, Woody

To get over my divorce, I got a prescription to live at the Playboy mansion for a while. ~ CAAN, James

She cried - and the judge wiped her tears with my checkbook. ~ MANVILLE, Tommy

I can't get divorced because I'm a Catholic. Catholics don't get divorced. They stay together through anger and hatred and festering misery, just like God intended. ~ CLARKE, Lenny

I look at divorce this way: it's better to have loved and lost, then to live with that bitch for the rest of my life. ~ MCGREW, Steve

Divorce

Marriage isn't all that it's cracked up to be. Let me tell you, honestly. Marriage is probably the chief cause of divorce.

~ GELBART, Larry

You know why divorces are so expensive? Because they're worth it.

~ NELSON, Willie

Congratulations on finalizing your divorce. You can now move on and begin a happier time in your life.

~ Anonymous

When two people decide to get a divorce, it isn't a sign that they "don't understand" one another, but a sign that they have, at last, begun to.

~ ROWLAND, Helen

Well done for finding the courage to begin your journey again. Be strong and have the confidence that happiness will come your way again.

~ Anonymous

Easter

Wishing you a happy Easter.
Celebrate the resurrection of Christ with your
family and friends.

~ Anonymous

Hope you have an egg-cellent time.

~ Anonymous

Rejoice in the resurrection and celebrate
new life. May you find peace and happiness
this Easter.

~ Anonymous

Father's Day

A father is someone who carries pictures in his wallet where his money used to be ~ Anonymous

When a father gives to his son, both laugh; when a son gives to his father, both cry ~ Anonymous

Fathers, be good to your daughters. You are the god and weight of her world ~ MAYOR, John

My father gave me the greatest gift anyone could give another person, he believed in me ~ VALVANO, Jim

Old as she was, she still missed her daddy sometimes ~ NAYLOR, Gloria

You know…fathers just have a way of putting everything together ~ COSBY, Erika

I cannot think of any need in childhood as strong as the need for a father's protection ~ FREUD, Sigmund

That is the thankless position of the father in the family-the provider for all, and the enemy of all ~ STRINDBERG, August

A father is always making his baby into a little woman. And when she is a woman he turns her back again ~ BAGNOLD, Enid

Why are men reluctant to become fathers? They aren't through being children ~ GARNER, Cindy

Father's Day

A father is a banker provided by nature ~ French proverb

A truly rich man is one whose children run into his arms when his hands are empty ~ Anonymous

Small boy's definition of Father's Day: It's just like Mother's Day only you don't spend so much ~ Anonymous

Never raise your hand to your kids, it leaves your groin unprotected ~ Red Buttons

Children have more need of models than critics. ~ JOUBERT, Joseph

Diogenes struck the father when the son swore. ~ BURTON, Robert

There must always be a struggle between a father and son, while one aims at power and the other at independence. ~ JOHNSON, Samuel

A man never stands as tall as when he kneels to help a child. ~ Knights of Pythagoras

The thing to remember about fathers is... they're men. A girl has to keep it in mind: They are dragon-seekers, bent on improbable rescues. Scratch any father, you find someone chock-full of qualms and romantic terrors, believing change is a threat, like your first shoes with heels on, like your first bicycle... ~ MCGINLEY, Phyllis

Father's Day

Be kind to thy father, for when thou wert young, Who loved thee so fondly as he? He caught the first accents that fell from thy tongue, And joined in thy innocent glee.

~ COURTNEY, Margaret

I talk and talk and talk, and I haven't taught people in 50 years what my father taught by example in one week.

~ CUOMO, Mario

Lucky that man whose children make his happiness in life and not his grief, the anguished disappointment of his hopes.

~ Euripedes

You don't have to deserve your mother's love. You have to deserve your father's. He's more particular.

~ FROST, Robert

Any man can be a Father but it takes someone special to be a dad

~ GEDDES, Anne

Fathers, like mothers, are not born. Men grow into fathers - and fathering is a very important stage in their development

~ GOTTESMAN, David M.

One father is more than a hundred schoolmasters

~ HERBERT, George

The father of a daughter is nothing but a high-class hostage. A father turns a stony face to his sons, berates them, shakes his antlers, paws the ground, snorts, runs them off into the underbrush, but when his daughter puts her arm over his shoulder and says, 'Daddy, I need to ask you something,' he is a pat of butter in a hot frying pan

~ KEILLOR, Garrison

My father didn't tell me how to live; he lived, and let me watch him do it.

~ KELLAND, Clarence Budington

Father's Day

When I was a kid, I said to my father one afternoon, 'Daddy, will you take me to the zoo?' He answered, 'If the zoo wants you, let them come and get you.

~ LEWIS, Jerry

Honour thy father and thy mother.

~ Matthew 19:19

A wise son maketh a glad father.

~ Proverbs 10:1

Sometimes the poorest man leaves his children the richest inheritance.

~ RENKEL, Ruth E.

That is the thankless position of the father in the family-the provider for all, and the enemy of all.

~ STRINDBERG, J. August

An angry father is most cruel towards himself.

~ Publilius Syrus

It's only when you grow up, and step back from him, or leave him for your own career and your own home—it's only then that you can measure his greatness and fully appreciate it. Pride reinforces love.

~ TRUMAN, Margaret

A man's children and his garden both reflect the amount of weeding done during the growing season

~ Anonymous

By the time a man realizes that maybe his father was right, he usually has a son who thinks he's wrong.

~ WADSWORTH, Charles

Father's Day

You know... fathers just have a way of putting everything together. ~ COSBY, Erika

A man knows when he is growing old because he begins to look like his father. ~ MARQUEZ, Gabriel Garcia

Don't make a baby if you can't be a father. ~ National Urban League Slogan

A man's desire for a son is usually nothing but the wish to duplicate himself in order that such a remarkable pattern may not be lost to the world. ~ ROWLAND, Helen

The worst misfortune that can happen to an ordinary man is to have an extraordinary father. ~ O'MALLEY, Austin

The father who does not teach his son his duties is equally guilty with the son who neglects them. ~ Confucius

Small boys become big men through the influence of big men who care about small boys. ~ Anonymous

You always believe in me even when I don't believe in myself. ~ Anonymous

Thank you Dad for giving me such a good start in life. You gave up so much for our happiness and for that I am truly blessed. ~ Anonymous

Friendship

It's much easier to turn a friendship into love, than love into friendship. ~ Anonymous

The worst solitude is to be destitute of sincere friendship. ~ BACON, Sir Francis

A real friend is someone who walks in when the rest of the world walks out. ~ Anonymous

I keep my friends as misers do their treasure, because, of all the things granted us by wisdom, none is greater or better than friendship. ~ ARETINO, Pietro

A tree is known by its fruit; a man by his deeds. A good deed is never lost; he who sows courtesy reaps friendship, and he who plants kindness gathers love. ~ Saint Basil the Great

There is no distance too far between friends, for friendship gives wings to the heart. ~ BENUDIZ, Kathy Kay

Friendship isn't a big thing - it's a million little things. ~ Anonymous

Friendships multiply joys and divide griefs. ~ BOHN, H. G.

Friendship is like money, easier made than kept. ~ BUTLER, Samuel

A friend who cannot at a pinch remember a thing or two that never happened is as bad as one who does not know how to forget. ~ BUTLER, Samuel

Friendship

Friendship without self-interest is one of the rare and beautiful things of life.   ~ BYRNES, James F.

A mistress never is nor can be a friend. While you agree, you are lovers; and when it is over, anything but friends.   ~ BYRON, Lord

Friendship is Love without his wings!   ~ BYRON, Lord

I have always laid it down as a maxim --and found it justified by experience --that a man and a woman make far better friendships than can exist between two of the same sex --but then with the condition that they never have made or are to make love to each other.   ~ BYRON, Lord

A friendship can weather most things and thrive in thin soil -- but it needs a little mulch of letters and phone calls and small silly presents every so often -- just to save it from drying out completely   ~ BROWN, Pam

Two persons cannot long be friends if they cannot forgive each other's little failings.   ~ Jean De La Bruyère

A good friend who points out mistakes and imperfections and rebukes evil is to be respected as if he reveals a secret of hidden treasure.   ~ Buddha

The rule of friendship means there should be mutual sympathy between them, each supplying what the other lacks and trying to benefit the other, always using friendly and sincere words.   ~ Buddha

Friendship

Friendship is a strong and habitual inclination in two persons to promote the good and happiness of one another.

~ BUDGELL, Eustace

Love is only chatter, friends are all that matter.

~ BURGESS, Gelett

Friendship is a sheltering tree.

~ COLERIDGE, Samuel Taylor

My true friends have always given me that supreme proof of devotion, a spontaneous aversion for the man I loved.

~ COLETTE, Sidonie Gabrielle

Friendship, of itself a holy tie, is made more sacred by adversity.

~ COLTON, Charles Caleb

True friendship is like sound health, the value of it is seldom known until it be lost.

~ COLTON, Charles Caleb

Of all things which wisdom provides to make life entirely happy, much the greatest is the possession of friendship.

~ Epicurus

Be more prompt to go to a friend in adversity than in prosperity.

~ Chilo

Every murderer is probably somebody's old friend.

~ CHRISTIE, Agatha

Life is nothing without friendship.

~ CICERO, Marcus T.

Every man can tell how many goats or sheep he possesses, but not how many friends.

~ CICERO, Marcus T.

Friendship

What sweetness is left in life, if you take away friendship?
Robbing life of friendship is like robbing the world of the sun. A
true friend is more to be esteemed than kinsfolk.

~ CICERO, Marcus T.

A friend is, as it were, a second self.

~ CICERO, Marcus T.

Friends are proved by adversity.

~ CICERO, Marcus T.

Don't walk in front of me, I may not follow; Don't walk behind me, I
may not lead; Walk beside me, and just be my friend.

~ CAMUS, Albert

Save me from the candid friend!

~ CANNING, George

Friendship is a pretty full-time occupation if you really are friendly
with somebody. You can't have too many friends because then
you're just not really friends.

~ CAPOTE, Truman

You can make more friends in two months by becoming interested
in other people than you can in two years by trying to get other
people interested in you.

~ CARNEGIE, Dale

Only solitary men know the full joys of friendship. Others have
their family --but to a solitary and an exile his friends are
everything.

~ CATHER, Willa

A man must eat a peck of salt with his friend, before he knows
him.

~ Miguel De Cervantes
1547-1616, Spanish
Novelist, Dramatist,
Poet

Friendship

The world is round so that friendship may encircle it. ~ Pierre Teilhard De Chardin

A friend hears the song in my heart and sings it to me when my memory fails. ~ Anonymous

Friendship is genuine when two friends can enjoy each others company without speaking a word to one another. ~ EBERS, George

Never exaggerate your faults, your friends will attend to that. ~ EDWARDS, Robert C.

Best friend, my well-spring in the wilderness! ~ ELIOT, George

What is a friend? I will tell you... it is someone with whom you dare to be yourself. ~ CRANE, Frank

A friend is one who knows us, but loves us anyway. ~ CUMMINGS, Fr. Jerome

Do not save your loving speeches for your friends till they are dead. Do not write them on their tombstones, speak them rather now instead. ~ CUMMINS, Anna

Then come the wild weather, come sleet or come snow, we will stand by each other, however it blow. ~ DACH, Simon

A man's friendships are one of the best measures of his worth. ~ DARWIN, Charles

Fate chooses our relatives, we choose our friends. ~ DELILLE, Jacques

Friendship

Do not have evil-doers for friends, do not have low people for   ~   Dhammapada
friends: have virtuous people for friends, have for friends the best
of men.

The most important things in life aren't things – but friends like   ~   Anonymous
you

One of the most difficult things to give away is kindness, it usually   ~   Anonymous
comes back to you.

The person who sows seeds of kindness, enjoys an everlasting   ~   Anonymous
harvest

If you must exercise, why not exercise kindness   ~   Anonymous

Love is blind; friendship closes its eyes   ~   Anonymous

"Should auld acquaintance be forgot   ~   BURNS, Robert
And never brought to mind?
We'll take a cup o'kindness yet,
For auld lang syne"

Your hearts, but not into each other's keeping.   ~   GIBRAN, Kahlil
For only the hand of Life can contain your hearts.
And stand together yet not too near together:
For the pillars of the temple stand apart,
And the oak tree and the cypress grow not in each other's
shadow.

Friendship

It is one of the blessings of old friends that you can afford to be stupid with them   ~   EMERSON, Ralph Waldo

Have no friends not equal to yourself   ~   Confucius

Keep your friendships in repair   ~   EMERSON, Ralph Waldo

Friendship is the only cement that will ever hold the world together   ~   WILSON, Woodrow

If you judge people, you have no time to love them   ~   Mother Teresa

Misfortune shows those who are not really friends   ~   Aristotle

Friendship is love without his wings   ~   BYRON, Lord

The best mirror is an old friend   ~   HERBERT, George

What is a friend? A single soul in two bodies   ~   Aristotle

A friendship that can cease has never been real   ~   Saint Jerome

A friend is, as it were, a second self   ~   Cicero

The world would be so lonely, in sunny hours or gray. Without the gift of friendship, to help us every day   ~   FARR, Hilda Brett

Friendship

Never shall I forget the days I spent with you. Continue to be my friend, as you will always find me yours ~ Ludwig van Beethoven

Walking with a friend in the dark is better than walking alone in the light ~ KELLER, Helen

Happiness is time spent with a friend and looking forward to sharing time with them again ~ WILKINSON, Lee

In the end, we will remember not the words of our enemies, but the silence of our friends ~ Martin Luther King Jr

Friendship is like a violin; the music may stop now and then, but the strings will last forever ~ Anonymous

Friends are the siblings God forgot to give us ~ Anonymous

Nothing makes the earth so spacious as to have friends at a distance ~ THOREAU, Henry David

No present could bring more joy to open than the one filled with your smile ~ Anonymous

I consider you my blood...it doesn't come any thicker! ~ Anonymous

I would rather you hate me for who I am than love me for who I'm not ~ Anonymous

Friendship

Through life we suffer. Through friends we never have to suffer alone   ~   Anonymous

Whoever said friendship is easy has obviously never had a true friend   ~   POLSON, Bronwyn

A real friend is one who walks in when the rest of the world walks out   ~   Anonymous

A friend is one who believes in you when you have ceased to believe in yourself   ~   Anonymous

Don't walk in front of me I may not follow.
Don't walk behind me, I may not lead.
Walk beside me and be my friend.   ~   CAMUS, Albert

I get by with a little help from my friends   ~   LENNON, John

The greatest good you can do for another is not just to share your riches, but to reveal to him his own   ~   DISRAELI, Benjamin

A friend is a gift you give yourself   ~   STEVENSON, Robert Louis

Truth and tears clears the way to a deep and lasting friendship   ~   SVIGN, Mariede

Misfortune shows those who are not really friends   ~   Aristotle

Friendship

A good friend is hard to find, hard to lose and impossible to forget ~ Anonymous

The best antiques are old friends ~ Anonymous

Friendship is not friendship without trust, without it I walk alone ~ James P. Michels jr.

Get Well

I just wanted you to know that I am thinking of you at this time. Try to stay strong and positive.   ~ Anonymous

A bowl of warmth, a soft embrace, a new day. Some get-well thoughts sent your way.   ~ Anonymous

An early morning walk is a blessing for the whole day.   ~ THOREAU, Henry David

As you rest and heal, know that you are thought of with great warmth and wished a quick recovery.   ~ Anonymous

Be careful when reading health books; you may die of a misprint.   ~ TWAIN, Mark

Get well cards have become so humorous that if you don't get sick you're missing half the fun.   ~ WILSON, Flip

Give yourself whatever gifts of time and rest you need to feel better - Get well soon.   ~ Anonymous

I enjoy convalescence. It is the part that makes the illness worthwhile.   ~ SHAW, George Bernard

I reckon being ill as one of the great pleasures of life, provided one is not too ill and is not obliged to work till one is better.   ~ BUTLER, Samuel

<u>Get Well</u>

I wonder why you can always read a doctor's bill and you can never read his prescription. ~ DUNNE, Finley Peter

Pain is inevitable. Suffering is optional. ~ CASEY, M. Kathleen

Sleep, riches, and health to be truly enjoyed must be interrupted. ~ RICHTER, Johann Paul Friedrich

The art of medicine consists of amusing the patient while nature cures the disease. ~ Voltaire

The best six doctors anywhere
And no one can deny it
Are sunshine, water, rest, and air
Exercise and diet.
These six will gladly you attend
If only you are willing
Your mind they'll ease
Your will they'll mend
And charge you not a shilling.
~ FIELDS, Wayne

The greatest healing therapy is friendship and love. ~ HUMPHREY, Hubert

There is no medicine like hope, no incentive so great, and no tonic so powerful as expectation of something tomorrow. ~ Orison Swett Marden

Time is the best doctor. ~ Yiddish Proverb

Warning: Humor may be hazardous to your illness. ~ KATZ, Ellie

Get Well

You have a cough? Go home tonight, eat a whole box of Ex-Lax - tomorrow you'll be afraid to cough. ~ WILLIAMS, Pearl

What's the use of worrying?
It never was worth while,
So, pack up your troubles in your old kit-bag,
And smile, smile, smile ~ ASAF, George

Troubles are often the tools by which God fashions us for better things ~ BEECHER, Henry Ward

It is better to light one small candle than to curse the darkness ~ Confucius

Every day in every way, I am getting better and better ~ COUE, Emily

Put a giant bandage where it hurts so everyone can see the pain you're in. ~ Anonymous

Eat right, exercise regularly, die anyway ~ Anonymous

My own prescription for health is less paperwork and more running barefoot through the grass ~ GRIMUTTER, Leslie

When an illness knocks you on your ass, you should stay down and relax for a while before trying to get up ~ CORE-STARKE, Candea

The most important thing in illness is never to lose heart ~ LENIN, Nikolai

Get Well

To avoid sickness eat less; to prolong life worry less

~ WENG,
Chu Hui

Going to University/College

"And seek for truth in the groves of Academe" ~ Horace

The larger the island of knowledge, the longer the shoreline of wonder ~ Anonymous

Nothing makes a little knowledge as dangerous as examination time ~ Anonymous

Some students drink at the fountain of knowledge, others just gargle ~ Anonymous

You may not know all the answers, but you probably won't be asked all the questions either ~ Anonymous

Knowledge is knowing a fact, wisdom is knowing what to do with that fact. ~ Anonymous

My father always told me, 'Find a job you love and you'll never have to work a day in your life. ~ FOX, Jim

Economists report that a college education adds many thousands of dollars to a man's lifetime income—which he then spends sending his children to college ~ VAUGHN, Bill

Education is an admirable thing, but it is well to remember from time to time that nothing worth knowing can be taught ~ WILDE, Oscar

You can lead a boy to college, but you cannot make him think ~ HUBBARD, Elbert

Going to University/College

Colleges don't make fools, they only develop them   ~ LORIMER, George

My schoolmates would make love to anything that moved, but I never saw any reason to limit myself   ~ PHILIPS, Emo

Education: the inculcation of the incomprehensible into the indifferent by the incompetent   ~ KEYNES, John Maynard

If you think education is expensive, try ignorance   ~ MCINTYRE, Andy

Leaving/Parting

A day without you is like a day without sunshine... I miss you... ~ Anonymous

Absence from whom we love is worse than death, and frustrates hope severer than despair. ~ COWPER, William

Absence makes the heart grow fonder. ~ Anonymous

Darkness isn't the absence of light... it's the absence of you. ~ Anonymous

Every parting is a form of death, as every reunion is a type of heaven. ~ EDWARDS, Tryon

I dropped a tear in the ocean. The day you find it is the day I will stop missing you. ~ Anonymous

I miss you like the sun misses the flowers, like the sun misses the flowers in the depths of winter, instead of beauty to direct it's light to, the heart hardens like the frozen world which your absence has banished me to. ~ Chaucer

I want to be in your arms, where you hold me tight and never let go. ~ Anonymous

If I never met you, I wouldn't like you. If I didn't like you, I wouldn't love you. If I didn't love you, I wouldn't miss you. But I did, I do, and I will. ~ Anonymous

If you think missing me is hard, then you should try missing you. ~ Anonymous

Leaving/Parting

I'm a fish out of water without you. ~ Anonymous

In the hope to meet
Shortly again, and make our absence sweet. ~ JONSON, Ben

Life is so short, so fast the lone hours fly,
We ought to be together, you and I. ~ ALFORD, Henry

Love is missing someone whenever you're apart, but somehow
feeling warm inside because you're close in heart. ~ KNUDSEN, Kay

Love reckons hours for months, and days for years; and every
little absence is an age. ~ DRYDEN, John

Missing someone gets easier every day because even though it's
one day further from the last time you saw each other, it's one day
closer to the next time you will. ~ Anonymous

Nothing makes the earth seem so spacious as to have friends at a
distance; they make the latitudes and longitudes. ~ THOREAU, Henry David

Parting is all we know of heaven and all we need to know of hell. ~ DICKINSON, Emily

Sometimes, when one person is missing, the whole world seems
depopulated. ~ Lamartine

Leaving/Parting

Somewhere there is someone that dreams of your smile, and finds in your presence that life is worthwhile, so when you are lonely remember it's true, someone somewhere is thinking of you. ~ Anonymous

The joy of meeting pays the pangs of absence; else who could bear it? ~ ROWE, Nicholas

When I go away from you
The world beats dead
Like a slackened drum.... ~ LOWELL, Amy

What shall I do with all the days and hours
That must be counted ere I see thy face?
How shall I charm the interval that lowers
Between this time and that sweet time of grace? ~ KEMBLE, Frances Anne

When I miss you, I don't have to go far ... I just have to look inside my heart because that's where I'll find you. ~ Ruthie

When you miss me just look up to the night sky and remember, I'm like a star; sometimes you can't see me, but I'm always there. ~ Jayde

When you're away, I miss you like a calm stream misses a breeze. ~ Anonymous

Where you used to be, there is a hole in the world, which I find myself constantly walking around in the daytime, and falling in at night. I miss you like hell. ~ MILLAY, Edna St. Vincent

Leaving/Parting

Within you I lose myself...
Without you I find myself
Wanting to be lost again.

~ Anonymous

Your absence has gone through me
Like thread through a needle
Everything I do is stitched with its colour.

~ MERWIN WS

Don't be dismayed at goodbyes. A farewell is necessary before
you can meet again. And meeting again, after moments or
lifetime, is certain for those who are friends.

~ BACH, Richard

We only part to meet again.

~ GAY, John

Why does it take a minute to say hello and forever to say
goodbye?

~ Anonymous

Gone - flitted away,
Taken the stars from the night and the sun
From the day!
Gone, and a cloud in my heart.

~ TENNYSON, Alfred

The world is round and the place which may seem like the end
may also be the beginning.

~ Ivy Baker Priest

May the road rise up to meet you, may the wind be ever at your
back. May the sun shine warm upon your face and the rain fall
softly on your fields. And until we meet again, may God hold you
in the hollow of his hand.

~ Irish Blessing

Leaving/Parting

Love is missing someone whenever you're apart, but somehow feeling warm inside because you're close in heart. ~ KNUDSEN, Kay

The reason it hurts so much to separate is because our souls are connected. ~ SPARKS, Nicholas

You and I will meet again
When we're least expecting it
One day in some far off place
I will recognize your face
I won't say goodbye my friend
For you and I will meet again

~ PETTY, Tom

Farewell! God knows when we shall meet again. ~ SHAKESPEARE, William

But fate ordains that dearest friends must part. ~ YOUNG, Edward

Where is the good in goodbye? ~ WILLSON, Meredith

Promise me you'll never forget me because if I thought you would I'd never leave ~ MILNE A.A.

May you always have work for your hands to do.
May your pockets hold always a coin or two.
May the sun shine bright on your windowpane.
May the rainbow be certain to follow each rain.
May the hand of a friend always be near you.
And may God fill your heart with gladness to cheer you.

~ Irish Blessing

Leaving/Parting

May the sun shine, all day long,
everything go right, and nothing wrong.
May those you love bring love back to you,
and may all the wishes you wish come true!

~ Irish Blessing

May you always have walls for the winds,
a roof for the rain, tea beside the fire,
laughter to cheer you, those you love near you,
and all your heart might desire.

~ Irish Blessing

A man never knows how to say goodbye; a woman never knows
when to say it.

~ ROWLAND, Helen

May you have warm words on a cool evening, a full moon on a
dark night, and a smooth road all the way to your door.

~ Irish Toast

If I had a single flower for every time I think about you, I could
walk forever in my garden.

~ GHANDI, Claudia

The best things said come last. People will talk for hours saying
nothing much and then linger at the door with words that come
with a rush from the heart.

~ ALDA, Alan

May flowers always line your path and sunshine light your day.
May songbirds serenade you every step along the way.
May a rainbow run beside you in a sky that's always blue.
And may happiness fill your heart each day your whole life
through.

~ Irish Blessing

Leaving/Parting

One kind kiss before we part,
Drop a tear, and bid adieu;
Though we sever, my fond heart
Till we meet shall pant for you.

~ DODSLEY, Robert

A sunbeam to warm you,
A moonbeam to charm you,
A sheltering angel, so nothing can harm you.

~ Irish Blessing

Where'er I roam, whatever realms to see,
My heart untravelled, fondly turns to thee;
Still to my brother turns, with ceaseless pain,
And drags at each remove a lengthening chain.

~ GOLDSMITH, Oliver

May brooks and trees and singing hills
Join in the chorus too,
And every gentle wind that blows
Send happiness to you.

~ Irish Blessing

I wanted a perfect ending. Now I've learned, the hard way, that
some poems don't rhyme, and some stories don't have a clear
beginning, middle, and end. Life is about not knowing, having to
change, taking the moment and making the best of it, without
knowing what's going to happen next.

~ RADNER, Gilda

Sweet is the memory of distant friends! Like the mellow rays of the
departing sun, it falls tenderly, yet sadly, on the heart.

~ Washington Irving

Goodbye, goodbye, I hate the word. Solitude has long since
turned brown and withered, sitting bitter in my mouth and heavy in
my veins.

~ GRENON, R.M.

Leaving/Parting

Missing someone gets easier every day because even though it's one day further from the last time you saw each other, it's one day closer to the next time you will. ~ Anonymous

Let's not unman each other - part at once;
All farewells should be sudden, when forever,
Else they make an eternity of moments,
And clog the last sad sands of life with tears. ~ BYRON, Lord

A goodbye isn't painful unless you're never going to say hello again. ~ Anonymous

Absence diminishes little passions and increases great ones, as the wind extinguishes candles and fans a fire. ~ Francois Duc de la Rochefoucauld,

Can miles truly separate you from friends.... If you want to be with someone you love, aren't you already there? ~ BACH, Richard

Don't be dismayed at goodbyes, a farewell is necessary before you can meet again and meeting again, after moments or lifetimes, is certain for those who are friends. ~ BACH, Richard

Don't cry because it's over. Smile because it happened. ~ SEUSS, Dr.

Goodbyes are not forever.
Goodbyes are not the end.
They simply mean I'll miss you
Until we meet again! ~ Anonymous

Leaving/Parting

Happy trails to you, until we meet again.
Some trails are happy ones,
Others are blue.
It's the way you ride the trail that counts,
Here's a happy one for you.

~ EVANS, Dale

People so seldom say I love you
And then it's either too late or love goes.
So when I tell you I love you,
It doesn't mean I know you'll never go,
Only that I wish you didn't have to.

~ Anonymous

Some people come into our lives
and leave footprints on our hearts
and we are never ever the same.

~ WEEDON, Flavia

You and I will meet again,
When we're least expecting it,
One day in some far off place,
I will recognize your face,
I won't say goodbye my friend,
For you and I will meet again.

~ PETTY, Tom

And the trouble is, if you don't risk anything, you risk even more

~ JONG, Erica

"If you don't know where you are going, you will probably end up somewhere else"

~ LAURENCE Dr. PETER J.

That's one small step for man, one giant leap for mankind

~ ARMSTRONG, Neil

Leaving/Parting

Always bear in mind that your own resolution to succeed is more important than any other one thing ~ LINCOLN, Abraham

No one can predict to what heights you can soar. Even you will not know until you spread your wings ~ Anonymous

You'll always miss 100% of the shots you don't take ~ Anonymous

The call of the wild ~ LONDON, Jack

Your new company is lucky to have you. You have always been a Tremendous Worker And Team player ~ Anonymous

Let's start kissing early, so the plane can leave on time ~ Anonymous

Loved one/Valentine

"I was nauseous and tingly all over.
I was either in love or I had smallpox." ~ ALLEN, Woody

My most brilliant achievement was my ability to be able to ~ CHURCHILL, Winston
persuade my wife to marry me.

To live without loving is to not really live. ~ Moliere

As sweet and musical ~ SHAKESPEARE,
As bright Apollo's lute, strung with his hair; William
And when Love speaks, the voice of all the gods
Makes heaven drowsy with the harmony.

Love is perhaps the only glimpse we are permitted of eternity. ~ HAYES, Helen

Two souls with but a single thought, ~ Franz Joseph van
Two hearts that beat as one. Munch Belling

We are shaped and fashioned by what we love. ~ Johann von Goethe

Husbands are like fires. They go out if unattended. ~ Zsa Zsa Gabor

The entire sum of existence is the magic of being needed ~ SMITH, Sydney
by just one person. To love and be loved is the greatest
happiness of existence.

Loved one/Valentine

I have great hopes that we shall love each other all our lives as much as if we had never married at all. ~ BYRON, Lord

I have found the paradox that if I love until it hurts, then there is no hurt, but only more love. ~ Mother Teresa

The last of your kisses was ever the sweetest; the last smile the brightest; the last movement the gracefullest. ~ KEATS, John

He is not a lover who does not love forever. ~ Euripides

When you love someone all your saved up wishes start coming out. ~ BOWEN, Elizabeth

You can't buy love, but you can pay heavily for it ~ YOUNGMAN, Henny

But there's nothing half so sweet in life As love's young dream. ~ MOORE, Thomas

He who love touches walks not in darkness. ~ Plato

Love never claims, it ever gives. ~ GANDHI, Mohandas K.

Love doesn't make the world go 'round. Love is what makes the ride worthwhile. ~ JONES, Franklin P.

Loved one/Valentine

Love is that condition in which the happiness of another person is essential to your own. ~ HEINLEIN, Robert A.

Love is composed of a single soul inhabiting two bodies. ~ Aristotle

If you love somebody, let them go, for if they return, they were always yours. And if they don't, they never were. ~ GIBRAN, Kahlil

And think not you can guide the course of love. For love, if it finds you worthy, shall guide your course. ~ GIBRAN, Kahil

We come to love not by finding the perfect person, but by learning to see an imperfect person perfectly. ~ KEEN, Sam

I recently read that love is entirely a matter of chemistry. That must be why my wife treats me like toxic waste. ~ BISSONETTE, David

Happiness is the china shop; love is the bull. ~ MENCK, H. L.

It is better to have loved and lost than never to have loved at all. ~ BUTLER, Samuel

Ever has it been that love knows not its own depth until the hour of separation. ~ GIBRAN, Kahlil

Real love stories never have endings. ~ BACH, Richard

Loved one/Valentine

Two souls and one thought, two hearts and one pulse.   ~ Halen

Immature love says: "I love you because I need you." Mature love says: "I need you because I love you.".   ~ FROMM, Erich

One advantage of marriage it seems to me is that when you fall out of love with him or he falls out of love with you it keeps you together until maybe you fall in again.   ~ VIORST, Judith

To love someone is to see a miracle invisible to others.   ~ MAUR, Francois

Try praising your wife, even if it does frighten her at first.   ~ SUNDAY, Billy

One man by himself is nothing.
Two people who belong together make a world.   ~ MARGOLIUS, Hans

We don't believe in rheumatism and true love until after the first attack!   ~ ESCHENBACH, Marie E.

The quarrels of lovers are like summer storms. Everything is more beautiful when they have passed.   ~ NECKER, Suzanne

They gave each other a smile with a future in it.   ~ LARDNER, Ring

Treasure each other in the recognition that we do not know how long we shall have each other.   ~ LIEBMAN, Joshua

Loved one/Valentine

Adieu,Adieu, kind friend adieu, adieu,adieu.   ~ Anonymous
I can no longer stay with you,
I'll hang my harp on a weeping willow tree,
And may the world go well with thee

I'll love you till the ocean   ~ AUDEN, W.H.
Is folded and hung up to dry
And the seven stars go squawking
Like geese about the sky

I love a lassie, a bonnie, bonnie lassie,   ~ LAUDER, Sir Harry
She's as pure as the lily in the dell.
She's as sweet as the heather, the bonnie bloomin' heather-
Mary, ma Scotch Bluebell

My dearest darling ducky,   ~ Anonymous
I love you clean and mucky,
But I love you best when you're undressed,
And ready for some nooky

I always say beauty is only sin deep   ~ Saki

There is love of course. And then there's life, its enemy   ~ ANOUILH, Jean

You know very well that love is, above all, the gift of oneself   ~ ANOUILH, Jean

Loved one/Valentine

Come to me in my dreams, and then
By day I shall be well again!
For then the night will more than pay
The hopeless longing of the day

~ ARNOLD, Matthew

Eternal passion!
Eternal pain

~ ARNOLD, Matthew

Resolve to be thyself: and know, that he
Who finds himself, loses his misery

~ ARNOLD, Matthew

When he was asked 'What is a friend?' He said 'One soul
inhabiting two bodies

~ Aristotle

Kissing a girl is like opening a jar of olives, hard to get the first
one, but the rest come easy

~ Anonymous

Anyone can be passionate, but it takes real lovers to be silly.

~ Franken, Rose

Anyone can catch your eye, but it takes someone special to catch
your heart.

~ Author Unknown

For twas not into my ear you whispered
But into my heart
Twas not my lips you kissed
But my soul

~ Garland, Judy

Loved one/Valentine

If love is so wonderful to give and of course.. to receive, why do   ~   Anonymous
we allow ourselves to allow outside influences to get us down?
Just go ahead and live in love! The more you love yourself and
others, the more you allow yourself to be loved.

If you have it [love]' you don't need to have anything else, and if   ~   Barrie, Sir James M.
you don't have it, it doesn't matter what else you have.

If it is your time, love will track you down like a cruise missile   ~   Barry, Lynda

Where love is concerned, too much is not even enough   ~   Pierre de
                                                                  Beaumarchais

Love fails, only when we fail to love.   ~   Franklin, J.

Love is a symbol of eternity. It wipes out all sense of time,   ~   Author Unknown
destroying all memory of a beginning and all fear of an end.

Love is an irresistible desire to be irresistibly desired.   ~   Frost, Robert

Love is friendship set on fire.   ~   Irons, Jeremy

Love is something you can't describe   ~   Anonymous
like the look of a rose,
the smell of the rain,
or the feeling of forever.

Love is the enchanted dawn of every heart.   ~   Lamartine

Loved one/Valentine

Love is the greatest refreshment in life.   ~ Pablo Picaso

Love is the master key that opens the gates of happiness.   ~ Holmes Oliver Wendell

Love makes your soul crawl out from its hiding place.   ~ Hurston, Zora Neale

Love unlocks doors and opens windows that weren't even there before.   ~ McLaughlin, Mignon

Love will find a way through paths where wolves fear to prey.   ~ Byron, Lord

Love would never be a promise of a rose garden unless it is showered with light of faith, water of sincerity and air of passion.   ~ Anonymous

The greatest science in the world; in heaven and on earth; is love.   ~ Mother Teresa

The heart that loves is always young.   ~ Anonymous

The hours I spend with you I look upon as sort of a perfumed garden, a dim twilight, and a fountain singing to it. You and you alone make me feel that I am alive. Other men it is said have seen angels, but I have seen thee and thou art enough.   ~ Moore, George

There is more hunger for love and appreciation in this world than for bread.   ~ Mother Teresa

Loved one/Valentine

We are all a little weird and life's a little weird, and when we find someone whose weirdness is compatible with ours, we join up with them and fall in mutual weirdness and call it love. ~ Anonymous

What the world really needs is more love and less paper work. ~ Bailey, Pearl

The best treat in this lifetime. ~ Westwood, Anna

Where there is great love there are always miracles. ~ Cather, Willa

You know when you have found your prince because you not only have a smile on your face but in your heart as well. ~ Anonymous

Love reckons hours for months, and days for years; and every little absence is an age. ~ Dryden, John

Promise me you'll never forget me because if I thought you would I'd never leave. ~ Milne, A.A.

Ever has it been that love knows not its own depth until the hour of separation. ~ Gibran, Kahlil

The return makes one love the farewell. ~ Alfred De Musset

If I had a single flower for every time I think about you, I could walk forever in my garden. ~ Ghandi, Claudia

Loved one/Valentine

Ye flowers that drop, forsaken by the spring,
Ye birds that, left by summer, cease to sing,
Ye trees that fade, when Autumn heats remove,
Say, is not absence death to those who love?

~ Pope, Alexander

The best things said come last. People will talk for hours saying
nothing much and then linger at the door with words that come
with a rush from the heart.

~ Alda, Alan

One kind kiss before we part,
Drop a tear, and bid adieu;
Though we sever, my fond heart
Till we meet shall pant for you.

~ Dodsley, Robert

I wanted a perfect ending. Now I've learned, the hard way, that
some poems don't rhyme, and some stories don't have a clear
beginning, middle, and end. Life is about not knowing, having to
change, taking the moment and making the best of it, without
knowing what's going to happen next.

~ Radner, Gilda

She went her unremembering way,
She went and left in me
The pang of all the partings gone,
And partings yet to be.

~ Thompson, Francis

Goodbye, goodbye, I hate the word. Solitude has long since
turned brown and withered, sitting bitter in my mouth and heavy in
my veins.

~ Grenon, R.M.

Missing someone gets easier every day because even though it's
one day further from the last time you saw each other, it's one day
closer to the next time you will.

~ Anonymous

Loved one/Valentine

Let's not unman each other - part at once;
All farewells should be sudden, when forever,
Else they make an eternity of moments,
And clog the last sad sands of life with tears.

~ Byron, Lord

Don't cry because it's over. Smile because it happened.

~ Geisel, Theodor
Seuss

Mothers Day

Mothers hold their children's hands for a short while, but their hearts forever   ~ Anonymous

A mother's arms are more comforting than anyone else's   ~ Diana, Princess of Wales

Being a full time mother is one of the highest salaried jobs...since the payment is pure love   ~ VERMONT, Mildred B.

No matter how old a mother is, she watches her middle-aged children for signs of improvement   ~ MAXWELL, Florida Scott

Whatever else is unsure in this stinking dunghill of a world a mother's love is not   ~ JOYCE, James

The real religion of the world comes from women much more than from men – from mothers most of all, who carry the key of our souls in their bosoms   ~ HOLMES, Oliver Wendell

Nobody knows of the work it makes
To keep the home together
Nobody knows of the steps it takes,
Nobody knows – but mother   ~ Anonymous

There is only one pretty child in the world, and every mother has it   ~ Chinese proverb

No gift to your mother can ever equal her gift to you   ~ Anonymous

Mothers Day

Setting a good example for your children takes all the fun out of middle age ~ FEATHER, William

Sorry I am unable to be with you this year to celebrate Mother's Day. My thoughts are with you and hope you have a wonderful day and don't miss me too much. Thank you for all that you do for me. ~ Anonymous

World's Best Mum! This says it all. You are a constant inspiration to me. ~ Anonymous

May our future together be as wonderful as our past ~ Anonymous

A mother is a person who seeing there are only four pieces of pie for five people, promptly announces she never did care for pie. ~ JORDAN, Tenneva

A suburban mother's role is to deliver children obstetrically once, and by car forever after. ~ Peter De Vries

The moment a child is born, the mother is also born. She never existed before. The woman existed, but the mother, never. A mother is something absolutely new. ~ Rajneesh

I remember my mother's prayers and they have always followed me. They have clung to me all my life. ~ LINCOLN, Abraham

Some mothers are kissing mothers and some are scolding mothers, but it is love just the same, and most mothers kiss and scold together. ~ BUCK, Pearl S.

Mothers Day

A Freudian slip is when you say one thing but mean your mother.   ~ Anonymous

Sweater, n.: garment worn by child when its mother is feeling chilly.   ~ BIERCE, Ambrose

Women's Liberation is just a lot of foolishness. It's the men who are discriminated against. They can't bear children. And no one's likely to do anything about that.   ~ MEIR, Golda

The heart of a mother is a deep abyss at the bottom of which you will always find forgiveness.   ~ Honoré de Balzac

All women become like their mothers. That is their tragedy. No man does. That's his.   ~ WILDE, Oscar

*Thou art thy mother's glass, and she in thee
Calls back the lovely April of her prime.*   ~ SHAKESPEARE, William

An ounce of mother is worth a pound of clergy.   ~ Spanish Proverb

When you are a mother, you are never really alone in your thoughts. A mother always has to think twice, once for herself and once for her child.   ~ LOREN, Sophia

If evolution really works, how come mothers only have two hands?   ~ BERLE, Milton

Mothers Day

Mothers are fonder than fathers of their children because they are more certain they are their own. ~ Aristotle

Motherhood has a very humanizing effect. Everything gets reduced to essentials. ~ STREEP, Meryl

The sweetest sounds to mortals given
Are heard in Mother, Home, and Heaven. ~ BROWN, William Goldsmith

My mom is a never ending song in my heart of comfort, happiness, and being. I may sometimes forget the words but I always remember the tune. ~ HARMON, Gracie

The formative period for building character for eternity is in the nursery. The mother is queen of that realm and sways a scepter more potent than that of kings or priests. ~ Anonymous

Mother love is the fuel that enables a normal human being to do the impossible. ~ GARRETTY, Marion C.

I love my mother as the trees love water and sunshine - she helps me grow, prosper, and reach great heights. ~ RADICI, Adabella

A mother is the truest friend we have, when trials heavy and sudden, fall upon us; when adversity takes the place of prosperity; when friends who rejoice with us in our sunshine desert us; when trouble thickens around us, still will she cling to us, and endeavour by her kind precepts and counsels to dissipate the clouds of darkness, and cause peace to return to our hearts. ~ Washington Irving

Mothers Day

Any mother could perform the jobs of several air traffic controllers with ease. ~ ALTHER, Lisa

That best academy, a mother's knee. ~ LOWELL, James Russell

A mother's arms are made of tenderness and children sleep soundly in them. ~ HUGO, Victor

Grown don't mean nothing to a mother. A child is a child. They get bigger, older, but grown? What's that suppose to mean? In my heart it don't mean a thing. ~ MORRISON, Toni

Hundreds of dewdrops to greet the dawn,
Hundreds of bees in the purple clover,
Hundreds of butterflies on the lawn,
But only one mother the wide world over. ~ COOPER, George

A mother's happiness is like a beacon, lighting up the future but reflected also on the past in the guise of fond memories. ~ Honoré de Balzac

A father may turn his back on his child, brothers and sisters may become inveterate enemies, husbands may desert their wives, wives their husbands. But a mother's love endures through all. ~ Washington Irving

A mom forgives us all our faults, not to mention one or two we don't even have. ~ BRAULT, Robert

Mothers Day

My mother is a poem
I'll never be able to write,
though everything I write
is a poem to my mother.

~ DOUBIAGO, Sharon

With what price we pay for the glory of motherhood.

~ DUNCAN, Isadora

One good mother is worth a hundred schoolmasters.

~ HERBERT, George

There's nothing like a mama-hug.

~ RADICI, Adabella

Who fed me from her gentle breast
And hushed me in her arms to rest,
And on my cheek sweet kisses prest?
My Mother.

~ TAYLOR, Anne

Mother's love is peace. It need not be acquired, it need not be
deserved.

~ FROMM, Erich

Who ran to help me when I fell,
And would some pretty story tell,
Or kiss the place to make it well?
My mother.

~ TAYLOR, Ann

Mother - that was the bank where we deposited all our hurts and
worries.

~ TALMAGE,
T. DeWitt

Mother is the name for God in the lips and hearts of little children.

~ THACKERAY, William
Makepeace

Mothers Day

A daughter is a mother's gender partner, her closest ally in the family confederacy, an extension of her self. And mothers are their daughters' role model, their biological and emotional road map, the arbiter of all their relationships.

~ SECUNDA, Victoria

Mother's love grows by giving.

~ LAMB, Charles

I miss thee, my Mother! Thy image is still The deepest impressed on my heart.

~ COOK, Eliza

The tie which links mother and child is of such pure and immaculate strength as to be never violated.

~ Washington Irving

I cannot forget my mother. [S]he is my bridge. When I needed to get across, she steadied herself long enough for me to run across safely.

~ WEEMS, Renita

A little girl, asked where her home was, replied, "where mother is."

~ BROOKS, Keith L.

Youth fades; love droops; the leaves of friendship fall; A mother's secret hope outlives them all.

~ HOLMES, Oliver Wendell

Most of all the other beautiful things in life come by twos and threes, by dozens and hundreds. Plenty of roses, stars, sunsets, rainbows, brothers and sisters, aunts and cousins, comrades and friends - but only one mother in the whole world.

~ WIGGIN, Kate Douglas

Mothers Day

If I was damned of body and soul,
I know whose prayers would make me whole,
Mother o' mine, O mother o'mine.

~ KIPLING, Rudyard

Whatever else is unsure in this stinking dunghill of a world a
mother's love is not.

~ JOYCE, James

My mother had a slender, small body, but a large heart - a heart so
large that everybody's joys found welcome in it, and hospitable
accommodation.

~ TWAIN, Mark

It's not easy being a mother. If it were easy, fathers would do it.

~ Anonymous

The mother's heart is the child's school room.

~ BEECHER, Henry Ward

Women know
The way to rear up children (to be just)
They know a simple, merry, tender knack
Of tying sashes, fitting baby shoes,
And stringing pretty words that make no sense,
And kissing full sense into empty words.

~ BROWNING, Elizabeth Barrett

My mom is literally a part of me. You can't say that about many
people except relatives, and organ donors.

~ LATET, Carrie

Every beetle is a gazelle in the eyes of its mother.

~ Moorish Proverb

All that I am or ever hope to be, I owe to my angel Mother.

~ LINCOLN, Abraham

Mothers Day

No painter's brush, nor poet's pen
In justice to her fame
Has ever reached half high enough
To write a mother's name.

~ Anonymous

A man's work is from sun to sun, but a mother's work is never done.

~ Anonymous

One lamp - thy mother's love - amid the stars
Shall lift its pure flame changeless, and before
The throne of God, burn through eternity -
Holy - as it was lit and lent thee here.

~ WILLIS, Nathaniel Parker

No one in the world can take the place of your mother. Right or wrong, from her viewpoint you are always right. She may scold you for little things, but never for the big ones.

~ TRUMAN, Harry

God could not be everywhere, so he created mothers.

~ Jewish Proverb

Life is the fruit she longs to hand you,
Ripe on a plate.
And while you live,
Relentlessly she understands you.

~ MCGINLEY, Phyllis

Because I feel that in the heavens above
The angels, whispering one to another,
Can find among their burning tears of love,
None so devotional as that of "Mother,"
Therefore, by that dear name I have long called you,
You who are more than mother unto me.

~ POE, Edgar Allan

Mothers Day

The best conversations with mothers always take place in silence, when only the heart speaks. ~ LATET, Carrie

Biology is the least of what makes someone a mother. ~ WINFREY, Oprah

A man loves his sweetheart the most, his wife the best, but his mother the longest. ~ Irish Proverb

I look back on my childhood and thank the stars above.
For everything you gave me, but mostly for your love ~ WINTERS, Wayne F.

I am not a perfect mother and I will never be.
You are not a perfect daughter and you will never be.
But put us together and we will be the best mother and daughter we would ever be. ~ PESANTE, Zoraida

A mother's love for her child is like nothing else in the world.
It knows no law, no pity,
it dares all things and crushes down remorselessly all that stands in its path. ~ CHRISTIE, Agatha

A mother is someone who dreams great dreams for you,
but then she lets you chase the
dreams you have for yourself and loves you just the same. ~ Anonymous

All that I am my mother made me. ~ ADAMS, John Quincy

Who is it that loves me and will love me forever with an affection which no chance, no misery, no crime of mine can do away?
It is you, my mother. ~ CARLYLE, Thomas

Mothers Day

Good family life is never an accident but always an achievement by those who share it. ~ BOSSARD, James H.

A mother is she who can take the place of all others but whose place no one else can take. ~ Cardinal Mermillod

What good mothers and fathers instinctively feel like doing for their babies is usually best after all. ~ SPOCK, Benjamin

Before you were conceived I wanted you. Before you were born I loved you. Before you were here an hour I would die for you. This is the miracle of life. ~ HAWKINS, Maureen

A mother is the one who is still there when everyone else has deserted you. ~ Anonymous

Of all the rights of women, the greatest is to be a mother. ~ YUTANG, Lin

Bitter are the tears of a child: Sweeten them.
Deep are the thoughts of a child: Quiet them.
Sharp is the grief of a child: Take it from him.
Soft is the heart of a child: Do not harden it. ~ GLENCONNER, Pamela

To understand your parents' love, you must raise children yourself. ~ Chinese Proverb

A mother is the truest friend we have, when trials, heavy and sudden, fall upon us when adversity takes the place of prosperity when friends who rejoice with us in our sunshine, desert us when ~ Washington Irving

Mothers Day

troubles thicken around us, still will she cling to us, and endeavor by her kind precepts and counsels to dissipate the clouds of darkness, and cause peace to return to our hearts.

A mother understands what a child does not say. ~ Anonymous

Mothers Day is in honour of the best Mother who ever lived - the Mother of your heart ~ JARVIS, Anna

A mother holds her children's hands for a while, their hearts forever. ~ Author Unknown

Sometimes the poorest woman leaves her children the richest inheritance. ~ RENKEL, Ruth E.

Once upon a memory someone wiped away a tear, held me close and loved me, Thank you, Mother dear. ~ Author Unknown

For the mother is and must be, whether she knows it or not, the greatest, strongest and most lasting teacher her children have. ~ SMITH, Hannah W.

A debt so large and special the like there is no other This debt and so much very more we owe it to our MOTHER! ~ RONAN, Bill

There is a religion in all deep love, but the love of a mother is the veil of a softer light between the heart and the heavenly Father. ~ COLERIDGE, Samuel Taylor

New Home

Where we love is home - home that our feet may leave, but not our hearts. ~ HOLMES, Sr. Oliver Wendell

Home, the spot of earth supremely blest,
A dearer, sweeter spot than all the rest. ~ MONTGOMERY, Robert

The ornaments of your house will be the guests who frequent it. ~ Anonymous

May the roof above us never fall in
And may we good companions beneath it never fall out. ~ Irish Blessing

The universe is merely a fleeting idea in God's mind - a pretty
uncomfortable thought, particularly if you've just made a down
payment on a house. ~ ALLEN, Woody

No man but feels more of a man in the world if he have but a bit of
ground that he can call his own. However small it is on the
surface, it is four thousand miles deep; and that is a very
handsome property. ~ Charles Dudley Warner

It takes hands to build a house, but only hearts can build a home. ~ Anonymous

Every house where love abides
And friendship is a guest,
Is surely home, and home sweet home
For there the heart can rest. ~ DYKE, Henry Van

New Home

People are living longer than ever before, a phenomenon undoubtedly made necessary by the 30-year mortgage.

~ LARSON, Doug

There's nothing to match curling up with a good book when there's a repair job to be done around the house.

~ RYAN, Joe

May your home always be too small to hold all of your friends.

~ Anonymous

And of all man's felicities
The very subtlest one, say I,
Is when for the first time he sees
His hearthfire smoke against the sky.

~ MORLEY, Christopher

The fellow that owns his own home is always just coming out of a hardware store.

~ HUBBARD, Frank McKinney

One only needs two tools in life: WD-40 to make things go, and duct tape to make them stop.

~ WEILACHER, G.M.

A perfect summer day is when the sun is shining, the breeze is blowing, the birds are singing, and the lawn mower is broken.

~ DENT, James

A house that does not have one worn, comfy chair in it is soulless.

~ SARTON, May

Old houses mended,
Cost little less than new before they're ended.

~ CIBBER, Colley

It's really the cat's house - we just pay the mortgage.

~ Anonymous

New Home

Hospitality is making your guests feel at home, even if you wish they were.   ~ Anonymous

I am grateful for the lawn that needs mowing, windows that need cleaning, and floors that need waxing because it means I have a home.   ~ Anonymous

Congratulations on your new home. May it be filled with happiness, laughter and good times.   ~ Anonymous

Promotion

Life allows us to ask for what we want, but usually gives us what we deserve ~ Anonymous

It horrifies me that ethics is only an optional extra at Harvard Business School ~ JONES, Sir John Harvey

Being good is good business ~ RODDICK, Anita

If you do things well, do them better. Be daring, be first, be different, be just ~ RODDICK, Anita

Have regard for your name, since it will remain for you longer than a great store of gold ~ Ecclesiasticus 41:122

If you do anything just for the money you don't succeed ~ HEARN, Barry

Everything comes to him who hustles while he waits ~ EDDISON, Thomas A.

Unless you are willing to drench yourself in your work beyond the capacity of the average person, you are just not cut out for positions at the top ~ PENNEY, J.C.

The only limits are, as always, those of vision ~ BROUGHTON, James

I think it is an immutable law in business that words are words, explanations are explanations, promises are promises - but only performance is reality ~ GENEEN, Harold

Promotion

It is my profound belief that a man or woman who rises up through the hierarchy of a corporation must justify his or her position every single day. They must also be in a state of perpetual anxiety, the healthy anxiety that makes one reject complacency

~ MAISONROUGE, Jacques

Contrary to the cliché, genuinely nice guys most often finish first or very near it

~ FORBES, Malcolm

In a hierarchy every employee tends to rise to his level of incompetence

~ LAURENCE Dr. PETER J.

Some succeed because they are destined to, but most because they are determined to

~ Anonymous

A racehorse that can run a mile a few seconds faster is worth twice as much. That little extra proves to be the greatest value

~ HESS, John D.

Power tends to corrupt and absolute power corrupts absolutely

~ ACTON, Lord

A friend in power is a lost friend

~ ADAMS, Henry Brooks

Nil carborundum illegitimi (Don't let the bastards grind you down)

~ Anonymous

Even though we can't have all we want, we ought to be thankful we don't get what we deserve

~ Anonymous

Retirement

Cheer up! The worst is yet to come!   ~ JOHNSON, Philander Chase

Let us, then, be up and doing,
With a heart for any fate;
Still achieving, still pursuing,
Learn to labour and to wait.   ~ LONGFELLOW, Henry Wadsworth

The trouble with retirement is that you never get a day off.   ~ LEMONS, Abe

When a man retires and time is no longer a matter of urgent importance, his colleagues generally present him with a watch.   ~ SHERRIFF, R.C.

When a man retires, his wife gets twice the husband but only half the income.   ~ RODRIGUEZ, Chi Chi

A retired husband is often a wife's full-time job.   ~ HARRIS, Ella

Retired is being twice tired, I've thought
First tired of working,
Then tired of not.   ~ ARMOUR, Richard

I've been attending lots of seminars in my retirement. They're called naps.   ~ BROWNWORTH, Merri

Retirement: It's nice to get out of the rat race, but you have to learn to get along with less cheese.   ~ PERRET, Gene

Retirement

I'm retired - goodbye tension, hello pension! ~ Anonymous

Retirement: World's longest coffee break. ~ Anonymous

Retirement has been a discovery of beauty for me. I never had the time before to notice the beauty of my grandkids, my wife, the tree outside my very own front door. And, the beauty of time itself. ~ JULE, Hartman

O, blest retirement! friend to life's decline -
How blest is he who crowns, in shades like these,
A youth of labor with an age of ease! ~ GOLDSMITH, Oliver

Life begins at retirement. ~ Anonymous

The challenge of retirement is how to spend time without spending money. ~ Author Unknown

If people concentrated on the really important things in life, there'd be a shortage of fishing poles. ~ LARSON, Doug

Retirement is wonderful. It's doing nothing without worrying about getting caught at it. ~ PERRET, Gene

Rest is not idleness, and to lie sometimes on the grass under trees on a summer's day, listening to the murmur of the water, or watching the clouds float across the sky, is by no means a waste of time. ~ LUBBOCK, J.

Retirement

The question isn't at what age I want to retire, it's at what income. ~ FOREMAN, George

Retirement means no pressure, no stress, no heartache... unless you play golf. ~ PERRET, Gene

I'm not just retiring from the company, I'm also retiring from my stress, my commute, my alarm clock, and my iron. ~ JULE, Hartman

Don't play too much golf. Two rounds a day are plenty. ~ VARDON, Harry

Don't simply retire from something; have something to retire to. ~ FOSDICK, Harry Emerson

I'm now as free as the breeze - with roughly the same income. ~ PERRET, Gene

Half our life is spent trying to find something to do with the time we have rushed through life trying to save. ~ ROGERS, Will

When you retire, you switch bosses - from the one who hired you to the one who married you. ~ PERRET, Gene

The money's no better in retirement but the hours are ~ Anonymous

When men reach their sixties and retire, they go to pieces. Women go right on cooking. ~ SHEEHY, Gail

There's never enough time to do all the nothing you want. ~ WATTERSON, Bill

Retirement

Age is only a number, a cipher for the records. A man can't retire his experience. He must use it.

~ BARUCH Bernard

A gold watch is the most appropriate gift for retirement, as its recipients have given up so many of their golden hours in a lifetime of service.

~ MAHTAR Harry

Don't underestimate the value of Doing Nothing, of just going along, listening to all the things you can't hear, and not bothering.

~ MILNE A.A.

Retire from work, but not from life.

~ SONI M.K.

Sometimes it's important to work for that pot of gold. But other times it's essential to take time off and to make sure that your most important decision in the day simply consists of choosing which colour to slide down on the rainbow.

~ PAGELS, Douglas

There must be quite a few things that a hot bath won't cure, but I don't know many of them.

~ PLATH, Sylvia

I enjoy waking up and not having to go to work. So I do it three or four times a day.

~ PERRET, Gene

In retirement, every day is Boss Day and every day is Employee Appreciation Day.

~ Anonymous

Retirement is like a long vacation in Las Vegas. The goal is to enjoy it the fullest, but not so fully that you run out of money.

~ CLEMENTS, Jonathan

Retirement

Retirement at sixty-five is ridiculous. When I was sixty-five I still had pimples.   ~ BURNS, George

You are only young once, but you can stay immature indefinitely.   ~ Anonymous

Youth would be an ideal state if it came a little later in life.   ~ ASQUITH, Herbert

Retirement is the ugliest word in the language.   ~ HEMINGWAY, Ernest

Golf is a day spent in a round of strenuous idleness.   ~ WORDSWORTH, William

First you forget names; then you forget faces; then you forget to zip up your fly; and then you forget to unzip your fly.   ~ RICKEY, Branch

In my retirement I go for a short swim at least once or twice every day. It's either that or buy a new golf ball.   ~ PERRET, Gene

Sometimes it's hard to tell if retirement is a reward for a lifetime of hard work or a punishment.   ~ Anonymous

The reason the pro tells you to keep your head down is so you can't see him laughing.   ~ DILLER, Phyllis

If you drink, don't drive. Don't even putt.   ~ MARTIN, Dean

Retirement

If you are going to throw a club, it is important to throw it ahead of you, down the fairway, so you don't have to waste energy going back to pick it up.   ~ BOLT, Tommy

Retirement kills more people than hard work ever did.   ~ FORBES, Malcolm

Retirement: That's when you return from work one day and say, "Hi, Honey, I'm home - forever.   ~ PERRET, Gene

Retire from work, but not from life.   ~ SONI, M. K.

The best time to start thinking about your retirement is before the boss does.   ~ Anonymous

Half our life is spent trying to find something to do with the time we have rushed through life trying to save.   ~ ROGERS, Will

It is time I stepped aside for a less experienced and less able man.   ~ ELLEDGE, Scott

When one door closes, another one opens, but we often look so long and regretfully at the closed door that we fail to see the one that has opened for us.   ~ BELL, Alexander Graham

There's one thing I always wanted to do before I quit...retire   ~ Groucho Marx

Retirement kills more people than hard work ever did   ~ FORBES, Malcolm

Retirement

The money's no better in retirement but the hours are   ~   Anonymous

I have never liked working. To me a job is an invasion of privacy   ~   MCGORTY, Danny

Retirement is wonderful. It's doing nothing without worrying about getting caught at it   ~   PERRET, Gene

I enjoy waking up and not having to go to work. So I do it three or four times a day.   ~   PERRET, Gene

A retired husband is often a wife's full-time job   ~   HARRIS, Ella

There's one thing I always wanted to do before I quit .... retire   ~   Groucho Marx

What do gardeners do when they retire?   ~   MONKHOUSE, Bob
Golfers never retire, they just lose their drive
Lumberjacks never retire, they just pine away
Accountants don't retire, they just lose their balance
Bank managers don't retire, they just lose interest
Vehicle mechanics? They re-tyre every day
Teachers don't retire, they just mark time
Roofers don't retire, they just wipe the slate clean
Engineers never retire, they just lose their bearings

Don't be dismayed at goodbyes. A farewell is necessary before you can meet again. And meeting again, after moments or lifetime, is certain for those who are friends.   ~   BACH Richard

Retirement

We only part to meet again.　　　　　　　　　　　　　～ GAY John

Man's feelings are always purest and most glowing in the hour of　～ RICHTER, Jean Paul
meeting and of farewell.

Why does it take a minute to say hello and forever to say　　　～ Anonymous
goodbye?

Nothing makes the earth seem so spacious as to have friends at a　～ THOREAU Henry
distance; they make the latitudes and longitudes.　　　　　　　David

Goodbyes are not forever.　　　　　　　　　　　　　　　　～ Anonymous
Goodbyes are not the end.
They simply mean I'll miss you
Until we meet again!

The world is round and the place which may seem like the end　　～ Ivy Baker Priest
may also be the beginning.

Absence from whom we love is worse than death, and frustrates　～ COWPER, William
hope severer than despair.

Excuse me, then! you know my heart;　　　　　　　　　　　～ GAY, John
But dearest friends, alas! must part.

May the road rise up to meet you, may the wind be ever at your　～ Irish Blessing
back. May the sun shine warm upon your face and the rain fall
softly on your fields. And until we meet again, may God hold you
in the hollow of his hand.

Retirement

Happy trails to you, until we meet again.
Some trails are happy ones,
Others are blue.
It's the way you ride the trail that counts,
Here's a happy one for you.

~ EVANS, Dale

No distance of place or lapse of time can lessen the friendship of those who are thoroughly persuaded of each other's worth.

~ SOUTHEY, Robert

Be well, do good work, and keep in touch.

~ KEILLOR, Garrison

You and I will meet again
When we're least expecting it
One day in some far off place
I will recognize your face
I won't say goodbye my friend
For you and I will meet again

~ PETTY, Tom

Farewell! God knows when we shall meet again.

~ SHAKESPEARE, William

In the hope to meet
Shortly again, and make our absence sweet.

~ JONSON, Ben

May you always have work for your hands to do.
May your pockets hold always a coin or two.
May the sun shine bright on your windowpane.
May the rainbow be certain to follow each rain.
May the hand of a friend always be near you.
And may God fill your heart with gladness to cheer you.

~ Irish Blessing

Retirement

May the sun shine, all day long,
everything go right, and nothing wrong.
May those you love bring love back to you,
and may all the wishes you wish come true!

~ Irish Blessing

May you always have walls for the winds,
a roof for the rain, tea beside the fire,
laughter to cheer you, those you love near you,
and all your heart might desire.

~ Irish Blessing

May you have warm words on a cool evening, a full moon on a
dark night, and a smooth road all the way to your door.

~ Irish Toast

The key to retirement is to find joy in the little things.

~ MILLER, Susan

Retirement, when every day is Saturday

~ Anonymous

Retirement: When you stop lying about your age and start lying
around the house.

~ Anonymous

Don't simply retire from something; have something to retire to.

~ FOSDICK, Harry Emerson

Retirement is a time when you never get around to doing all those
things you intended to do when working

~ Anonymous

There are more pleasant things to do than beat up people.

~ ALI, Muhammad

Retirement

Retirement is wonderful if you have two essentials — much to live on and much to live for. ~ Anonymous

Retirement kills more people than hard work ever did. ~ FORBES, Malcolm

Age (and retirement) appear to be best in four things — old wood best to burn, old wine to drink, old friends to trust, and old authors to read. ~ BACON, Francis

There are so many other interesting ways to spend your time. I feel like early retirement is a gift, but it's such an incredible gift. It's a gift I need to use. ~ FELT-BARDON, Martha

The money's no better in retirement but the hours are! ~ Anonymous

Absence diminishes little passions and increases great ones, as the wind extinguishes candles and fans a fire. ~ Francois Duc de la Rochefoucauld

Sorry

Can you please forgive me. I was not thinking and said things that hurt you, for that I am truly sorry.   ~ Anonymous

I'm sorry I hurt your feelings and hope that someday you will find it in your heart to forgive me.   ~ Anonymous

I was a fool to let you go without a fight, is there any chance you will forgive me? You mean the world to me.   ~ Anonymous

What I did, I regret
So lets make up and forget.   ~ Anonymous

I'm sorry that I'm not perfect
I'm sorry for the tears that you cried
I'm sorry for the pain I caused
I'm sorry that lied   ~ Anonymous

When you realize you've made a mistake, make amends immediately.
It's easier to eat crow while it's still warm.   ~ HEIST, Dan

An apology is the superglue of life. It can repair just about anything.   ~ JOHNSTON, Lynn

It is a good rule in life never to apologize.
The right sort of people do not want apologies,
and the wrong sort take a mean advantage of them.   ~ WODEHOUSE, P.G.

Sorry

Never ruin an apology with an excuse.   ~ Anonymous

If it's a good idea, go ahead and do it.
It's much easier to apologize than it is to get permission.   ~ HOPPER, Grace

Right actions in the future are the best apologies for bad actions
in the past.   ~ EDWARDS, Tryon

Keep your words soft and tender because tomorrow you may have
to eat them.   ~ Author Unknown

Never ruin an apology with an excuse.   ~ JOHNSON, Kimberly

In some families, please is described as the magic word. In our
house, however, it was sorry.   ~ LAURENCE, Margaret

True remorse is never just a regret over consequence; it is a
regret over motive.   ~ MCLAUGHLIN, Mignon

There's one sad truth in life I've found
While journeying east and west -
The only folks we really wound
Are those we love the best.
We flatter those we scarcely know,
We please the fleeting guest,
And deal full many a thoughtless blow
To those who love us best.   ~ WILCOX, Ella Wheeler

Forgiveness is the sweetest revenge.   ~ FRIEDMANN, Isaac

Sorry

An apology is a good way to have the last word. ~ Anonymous

Forgiveness does not change the past, but it does enlarge the future. ~ BOESE, Paul

Remember, we all stumble, every one of us. That's why it's a comfort to go hand in hand. ~ KIMBROUGH, Emily

It's easier to ask forgiveness than it is to get permission. ~ HOPPER, Grace

If you were going to die soon and had only one phone call you could make, who would you call and what would you say? And why are you waiting? ~ LEVINE, Stephen

For every minute you are angry, you lose sixty seconds of happiness. ~ Anonymous

Not the fastest horse can catch a word spoken in anger. ~ Chinese Proverb

It is easier to forgive an enemy than to forgive a friend. ~ BLAKE, William

True friends stab you in the front. ~ WILDE, Oscar

The most important trip you may take in life is meeting people halfway. ~ BOYE, Henry

Thankyou

It isn't what you have in your pocket that makes you thankful, but what you have in your heart. ~ Anonymous

One can pay back the loan of gold, but one dies forever in debt to those who are kind. ~ Malayan Proverb

Unselfish and noble actions are the most radiant pages in the biography of souls. ~ THOMAS, David

Not what we give,
But what we share,
For the gift
without the giver
Is bare.

~ LOWELL, James Russell

Silent gratitude isn't much use to anyone. ~ STERN, G.B.

I can no other answer make, but, thanks, and thanks. ~ SHAKESPEARE, William

The only people with whom you should try to get even are those who have helped you. ~ SOUTHARD, John E.

I would maintain that thanks are the highest form of thought, and that gratitude is happiness doubled by wonder. ~ G.K. Chesterton

I would thank you from the bottom of my heart, but for you my heart has no bottom. ~ Anonymous

Thankyou

The smallest act of kindness is worth more than the grandest intention. ~ WILDE, Oscar

Gratitude is the memory of the heart. ~ MASSIEU, Jean Baptiste

How far that little candle throws his beams!
So shines a good deed in a naughty world. ~ SHAKESPEARE, William

It's nice to be important, but it's more important to be nice. ~ Anonymous

Kindness is the language which the deaf can hear and the blind can see. ~ TWAIN, Mark

How beautiful a day can be
When kindness touches it! ~ ELLISTON, George

We can only be said to be alive in those moments when our hearts are conscious of our treasures. ~ WILDER, Thornton

I feel a very unusual sensation - if it is not indigestion, I think it must be gratitude. ~ DISRAELI, Benjamin

Hem your blessings with thankfulness so they don't unravel. ~ Anonymous

Thank you for the days, those endless days, you gave me. ~ Anonymous

Thankyou

As we express our gratitude, we must never forget that the highest appreciation is not to utter words, but to live by them. ~ KENNEDY, John F.

If the only prayer you ever say in your entire life is 'thank you', it will be enough. ~ Meister Eckhart

I would maintain that thanks are the highest form of thought, and that gratitude is happiness doubled by wonder. ~ G.K. Chesterton

God gave you a gift of 86,400 seconds today. Have you used one to say "thank you? ~ WARD, William Arthur

Give thanks for a little and you will find a lot. ~ The Hausa of Nigeria

Make it a habit to tell people thank you. To express your appreciation, sincerely and without the expectation of anything in return. Truly appreciate those around you, and you'll soon find many others around you. Truly appreciate life, and you'll find that you have more of it. ~ MARSTON, Ralph

The depth and the willingness with which we serve is a direct reflection of our gratitude. ~ WATTS, Gordon T.

Every time we remember to say "thank you", we experience nothing less than heaven on earth. ~ BREATHNACH, Sarah Ban

Feeling gratitude and not expressing it is like wrapping a present and not giving it. ~ WARD, William Arthur

Thankyou

Thankfulness is the beginning of gratitude. Gratitude is the completion of thankfulness. Thankfulness may consist merely of words. Gratitude is shown in acts.   ~ MCKAY, David O.

For your thoughtfulness and generosity, from you I have learned much of life's philosophy Thank you sincerely.   ~ Anonymous

Get down on your knees and thank God you're still on your feet."   ~ Anonymous

Blessed are those that can give without remembering and receive without forgetting.   ~ Anonymous

To educate yourself for the feeling of gratitude means to take nothing for granted, but to always seek out and value the kind that will stand behind the action. Nothing that is done for you is a matter of course. Everything originates in a will for the good, which is directed at you. Train yourself never to put off the word or action for the expression of gratitude.   ~ SCHWEITZER, Albert

What if you gave someone a gift, and they neglected to thank you for it - would you be likely to give them another? Life is the same way. In order to attract more of the blessings that life has to offer, you must truly appreciate what you already have.   ~ MARSTON, Ralph

No duty is more urgent than that of returning thanks.   ~ Anonymous

A thankful person is thankful under all circumstances. A complaining soul complains even if he lives in paradise.   ~ Baha'u'llah

Thankyou

What we have done for ourselves alone dies with us; what we have done for others and the world remains and is immortal.

~ PIKE, Albert

Saying "thank you" creates love.

~ KINGMA, Daphne Rose

"You simply will not be the same person two months from now after consciously giving thanks each day for the abundance that exists in your life. And you will have set in motion an ancient spiritual law: the more you have and are grateful for, the more will be given you.

~ BREATHNACH, Sarah Ban

A thankful heart is not only the greatest virtue, but the parent of all other virtues.

~ Cicero

Gratitude makes sense of our past, brings peace for today, and creates a vision for tomorrow

~ Melody Beattie

None is more impoverished than the one who has no gratitude. Gratitude is a currency that we can mint for ourselves, and spend without fear of bankruptcy.

~ Fred De Witt Van Amburgh

The roots of all goodness lie in the soil of appreciation for goodness.

~ The Dalai Lama

Two kinds of gratitude: The sudden kind we feel for what we take; the larger kind we feel for what we give.

~ ROBINSON, Edwin Arlington

Thankyou

No one who achieves success does so without acknowledging the help of others. The wise and confident acknowledge this help with gratitude. ~ Anonymous

Gratitude is when memory is stored in the heart and not in the mind. ~ HAMPTON, Lionel

Gratitude is the best attitude. There is not a more pleasing exercise of the mind than gratitude. It is accompanied with such an inward satisfaction that the duty is sufficiently rewarded by the performance. ~ ADISSON, Joseph

Thank you for the good times,
The days you filled with pleasure.
Thank you for fond memories,
And for feelings I'll always treasure ~ FUCHS, Karl

Appreciation is a wonderful thing. It makes what is excellent in others belong to us as well. ~ Voltaire

Wherever there is a human being, there is an opportunity for a kindness. ~ Seneca

Kindness, like a boomerang, always returns. ~ Anonymous

When a person doesn't have gratitude, something is missing in his or her humanity. A person can almost be defined by his or her attitude toward gratitude. ~ WIESEL, Elie

Thankyou

Those who bring sunshine to the lives of others cannot keep it from themselves.

~ BARRIE, James Matthew

I thank you for your kindness,
I will not soon forget;
You're one of the nicest people
I have ever met.....

~ FUCHS, Joanna

Wedding

A good marriage is that in which each appoints the other guardian of his solitude. ~ RILKE, Rainer Maria

A successful marriage requires falling in love many times, always with the same person. ~ GREER, Germaine

Are we not like two volumes of one book? ~ Marceline Desbordes-Valmore

Grow old with me! The best is yet to be. ~ BROWNING, Robert

Happy and thrice happy are those who enjoy an uninterrupted union, and whose love, unbroken by any sour complaints, shall not dissolve until the last day of their existence. ~ Horace

I love being married. It's so great to find that one special person you want to annoy for the rest of your life. ~ RUDNER, Rita

In all of the wedding cake, hope is the sweetest of plums. ~ JERROLD, Douglas

In marriage, everyday you love, and everyday you forgive. It is an ongoing sacrament, love and forgiveness. ~ MOYERS, Bill

Marriage--a book of which the first chapter is written in poetry and the remaining chapters written in prose. ~ NICHOLS, Beverly

Marriage is an Athenic weaving together of families, of two souls with their individual fates and destinies, of time and eternity-- everyday life married to the timeless mysteries of the soul. ~ MOORE, Thomas

Wedding

Marrying a man is like buying something you've been admiring for a long time in a shop window. You may love it when you get home, but it doesn't always go with everything else in the house. ~ KERR, Jean

Now join hands, and with your hands your hearts. ~ SHAKESPEARE, William

The sum which two married people owe to one another defies calculation. It is an infinite debt, which can only be discharged through all eternity. ~ Johann Wolfgang von Goethe

There is no more lovely, friendly and charming relationship, communion or company than a good marriage. ~ LUTHER, Martin

There is nothing nobler or more admirable than when two people who see eye to eye keep house as man and wife, confounding their enemies and delighting their friends. ~ Homer

This day I will marry my friend, the one I laugh with, live for, dream with, love. ~ Anonymous

To have and to hold from this day forward, for better or worse, for richer for poorer, in sickness and in health, to love and to cherish till death do us part. ~ Book of Common Prayer

To keep your marriage brimming, with love in the wedding cup, whenever you're wrong, admit it; whenever you're right, shut up. ~ NASH, Ogden

Two souls with but a single thought,
Two hearts that beat as one. ~ HALM, Friedrich

Wedding

Two such as you with such a master speed cannot be parted nor be swept away from one another once you are agreed that life is only life forevermore together wing to wing and oar to oar.   ~ FROST, Robert

We've got this gift of love, but love is like a precious plant. You can't just accept it and leave it in the cupboard or just think it's going to get on by itself. You've got to keep watering it. You've got to really look after it and nurture it.   ~ LENNON, John

Whatever souls are made of, his and mine are the same.   ~ BRONTE, Emily

When you make a sacrifice in marriage, you're sacrificing not to each other but to unity in a relationship.   ~ CAMPBELL, Joseph

When you meet someone who can cook and do housework--don't hesitate a minute--marry him.   ~ Anonymous

I had bad luck with both my wives. The first one left me and the second one didn't   ~ MURRAY, Patrick

Love is temporary insanity curable by marriage   ~ BIERCE, Ambrose

My wife is a sex object – every time I ask for sex she objects.   ~ DAWSON, Les

A successful man is one who makes more money than his wife can spend. A successful woman is one who can find such a man   ~ TURNER, Lana

I married beneath me. All women do   ~ ASTOR, Nancy

Wedding

The ideal marriage consists of a deaf husband and a blind wife ~ COLUM, Padraig

May today be the beginning of a long and beautiful journey. ~ Anonymous
Wishing you all the very best for your new life together.

What a privilege to be here with you to share this special day. ~ Anonymous
Such lovely people deserve the very best in life.
Wishing you a long and happy future together.

May your new life together be filled with love, ~ Anonymous
happiness and harmony. We wish you well.

Remember, a woman worries about the future until she meets a ~ Anonymous
husband. A man doesn't worry about the future until he meets his
wife

Treat a dog with kindness, pet him often, feed him well, and he'll ~ Anonymous
never leave you. The same system usually works with husbands

Bigamy is having one husband too many. Monogamy is the same ~ JONG, Erica

Hark! The merry chimes are pealing, ~ COOK, Eliza
Soft and glad the music swells,
Gaily in the night wind stealing,
Sweetly sound the wedding bells.

Men always want to be a woman's first love. Women have a more ~ WILDE, Oscar
subtle instinct: What they like is to be a man's last romance.

Wedding

All marriages are happy. It's living together afterwards that is difficult.   ~ Anonymous

I told my wife that a husband is like a fine wine; he gets better with age. The next day, she locked me in the cellar.   ~ Anonymous

If it weren't for marriage, men and women would have to fight with total strangers.   ~ Anonymous

If it weren't for marriage, men would spend their lives thinking they had no faults at all.   ~ Anonymous

Is it better for a woman to marry a man who loves her than a man she loves. If she's lucky she can have both.   ~ Anonymous

Marital Freedom: The liberty that allows a husband to do exactly that which his wife pleases.   ~ Anonymous

Marriage is a romance in which the hero dies in the first chapter.   ~ Anonymous

Mother-in-law: A woman who destroys her son-in-law's peace of mind by giving him a piece of hers.   ~ Anonymous

Some men are born with cold feet; some acquire cold feet; and some have cold feet thrust upon them.   ~ Anonymous

We come to love not by finding the perfect person, but by learning to see an imperfect person perfectly.   ~ KEEN, Sam

Wedding

The trouble with some women is that they get all excited about nothing, and then marry him   ~ Cher

The secret of a happy marriage remains a secret!   ~ YOUNGMAN, Henry

Before marriage a man will lay awake all night thinking about something you said; after marriage he'll fall asleep before you have finished saying it.   ~ ROWLAND, Helen

An archaeologist is the best husband a woman can have. The older she gets, the more interested he is in her.   ~ CHRISTIE, Agatha

Marriage is a wonderful institution, but who wants to live in an institution?   ~ Groucho Marx

Marriage is popular because it combines the maximum of temptation with the maximum of opportunity.   ~ SHAW, George Bernard

The most dangerous food a man can eat is wedding cake.   ~ Anonymous

A man in love is incomplete until he is married. Then he's finished   ~ Anonymous

Marriage requires a person to prepare 4 types of "Rings": Engagement Ring Wedding Ring, Suffering, Enduring   ~ Anonymous

They have come up with a perfect understanding. He won't try to run her life, and he won't try to run his, either.   ~ Anonymous

Wedding

Marriage is like a hot bath. Once you get used to it, it's not so hot. ~ Anonymous

He early on let her know who is the boss. He looked her right in the eye and clearly said, "You're the boss." ~ Anonymous

The woman cries before the wedding; the man afterward. ~ Anonymous

Every mother generally hopes that her daughter will snag a better husband than she managed to do...but she's certain that her boy will never get as great a wife as his father did. ~ Anonymous

Compromise: An amiable arrangement between husband and wife whereby they agree to let her have her own way. ~ Anonymous

The path that leads to happiness is so narrow that two cannot walk on it unless they have become one. ~ Anonymous

Take a generous dose of love ~ Anonymous
Add a measure or two of respect
Mix in some co-operation
Stir with the spoon of kindness
Add a dash of affection
A cuddle or two to taste
And a goodly dollop of humour
Sprinkle on tolerance and patience
Bake it in a bowl of friendship
And what have you got?
Your marriage through the years

BEECHER	Henry Ward	BABY/CHRISTENING	9
BEECHER	Henry Ward	GET WELL	68
BEECHER	Henry Ward	MOTHERS DAY	100
BELL	Alexander Graham	RETIREMENT	115
BENNETT	Dan	BIRTHDAY	27
BENNY	Jack	BIRTHDAY	19
BENNY	Jack	BIRTHDAY	29
BENUDIZ	Kathy Kay	FRIENDSHIP	56
BERGMAN	Ingrid	BIRTHDAY	29
BERLE	Milton	BABY/CHRISTENING	10
BERLE	Milton	MOTHERS DAY	95
BIERCE	Ambrose	MOTHERS DAY	95
BIERCE	Ambrose	WEDDING	133
BISSONETTE	David	LOVED ONE/VALENTINE	84
BLAKE	William	SORRY	123
BLAKELEY	Mary K	DIVORCE	48
BLOOMINGDALE	Theresa	BABY/CHRISTENING	10
BOESE	Paul	SORRY	123
BOHN	H. G.	FRIENDSHIP	56
BOLT	Tommy	RETIREMENT	115
BOSSARD	James H.	MOTHERS DAY	103
BOWEN	Elizabeth	LOVED ONE/VALENTINE	83
BOYE	Henry	SORRY	123
BRAULT	Robert	MOTHERS DAY	97
BREATHNACH	Sarah Ban	THANKYOU	126
BREATHNACH	Sarah Ban	THANKYOU	128
BRONTE	Emily	WEDDING	133
BROOKS	Norman W.	CHRISTMAS	32
BROOKS	Keith L.	MOTHERS DAY	99
BROOKS	Phillips	CHRISTMAS	36
BROOKS	Phillips	CHRISTMAS	38
BROOKS	Phillips	CHRISTMAS	38
BROOKS	Phillips	CHRISTMAS	42
BROUGHTON	James	PROMOTION	108
BROWN	H. Jackson	CONGRATULATIONS	46
BROWN	Jr H. Jackson	BABY/CHRISTENING	11
BROWN	Pam	FRIENDSHIP	57
BROWN	William Goldsmith	MOTHERS DAY	96
BROWNING	Elizabeth Barrett	MOTHERS DAY	100
BROWNING	Robert	BIRTHDAY	26
BROWNING	Robert	WEDDING	131
BROWNWORTH	Merri	RETIREMENT	110
BRUYERE (De La)	Jean	FRIENDSHIP	57
BUCK	Pearl S.	MOTHERS DAY	94
BUDDHA	Buddha	FRIENDSHIP	57
BUDDHA	Buddha	FRIENDSHIP	57
BUDGELL	Eustace	FRIENDSHIP	58
BURGESS	Gelett	FRIENDSHIP	58
BURKE	Leo J.	BABY/CHRISTENING	9
BURNS	George	RETIREMENT	114
BURNS	Robert	FRIENDSHIP	61
BURTON	Robert	FATHERS DAY	52
BUTLER	Samuel	FRIENDSHIP	56
BUTLER	Samuel	FRIENDSHIP	56
BUTLER	Samuel	GET WELL	66
BUTLER	Samuel	GET WELL	68
BUTLER	Samuel	LOVED ONE/VALENTINE	84
BUXBAUM	Martin	BIRTHDAY	24
BYRNES	James F.	FRIENDSHIP	57
BYRON	Lord	FRIENDSHIP	57
BYRON	Lord	FRIENDSHIP	57
BYRON	Lord	FRIENDSHIP	57

BYRON	Lord	FRIENDSHIP	62
BYRON	Lord	LEAVING/PARTING	79
BYRON	Lord	LOVED ONE/VALENTINE	83
BYRON	Lord	LOVED ONE/VALENTINE	89
BYRON	Lord	LOVED ONE/VALENTINE	92
CAAN	James	DIVORCE	48
CALDWELL	Taylor	CHRISTMAS	37
CAMERON	W. J.	CHRISTMAS	33
CAMERON	W. J.	CHRISTMAS	35
CAMPBELL	Joseph	WEDDING	133
CAMUS	Albert	FRIENDSHIP	59
CAMUS	Albert	FRIENDSHIP	64
CANNING	George	FRIENDSHIP	59
CAPOTE	Truman	FRIENDSHIP	59
CARDINAL	Mermillod	MOTHERS DAY	103
CARLYLE	Thomas	MOTHERS DAY	102
CARNEGIE	Dale	FRIENDSHIP	59
CARROLL	Lewis	BIRTHDAY	26
CASEY	M. Kathleen	GET WELL	67
CATHER	Willa	FRIENDSHIP	59
CATHER	Willa	LOVED ONE/VALENTINE	90
CHALMERS	Irena	BABY/CHRISTENING	11
CHANEL	Coco	BIRTHDAY	24
CHASE	Mary Ellen	CHRISTMAS	33
CHASE	Mary Ellen	CHRISTMAS	36
CHAUCER	Chaucer	LEAVING/PARTING	72
CHER	Cher	WEDDING	136
CHEVALIER	Maurice	BIRTHDAY	22
CHILO	Chilo	FRIENDSHIP	58
CHRISTIE	Agatha	FRIENDSHIP	58
CHRISTIE	Agatha	MOTHERS DAY	102
CHRISTIE	Agatha	WEDDING	136
CHURCHILL	Winston	LOVED ONE/VALENTINE	82
CIBBER	Colley	NEW HOME	106
CICERO	Cicero	FRIENDSHIP	62
CICERO	Cicero	THANKYOU	128
CICERO	Marcus T.	FRIENDSHIP	58
CICERO	Marcus T.	FRIENDSHIP	58
CICERO	Marcus T.	FRIENDSHIP	59
CICERO	Marcus T.	FRIENDSHIP	59
CICERO	Marcus T.	FRIENDSHIP	59
CLARK	Frank A.	BABY/CHRISTENING	11
CLARKE	Lenny	DIVORCE	48
CLEMENCEAU	Georges	BIRTHDAY	27
CLEMENTS	Jonathan	RETIREMENT	113
COFFIN	Harold	BIRTHDAY	27
COLERIDGE	Samuel Taylor	BABY/CHRISTENING	12
COLERIDGE	Samuel Taylor	FRIENDSHIP	58
COLERIDGE	Samuel Taylor	MOTHERS DAY	104
COLETTE	Sidonie Gabrielle	FRIENDSHIP	58
COLTON	Charles Caleb	FRIENDSHIP	58
COLTON	Charles Caleb	FRIENDSHIP	58
COLUM	Padraig	WEDDING	134
COOK	Eliza	MOTHERS DAY	99
COOK	Eliza	WEDDING	134
COOPER	George	MOTHERS DAY	97
CORE-STARKE	Candea	GET WELL	68
COSBY	Bill	BABY/CHRISTENING	13
COSBY	Erika	FATHERS DAY	51
COSBY	Erika	FATHERS DAY	55
COUE	Emily	GET WELL	68
COURTNEY	Margaret	FATHERS DAY	53

COWPER	William	LEAVING/PARTING	72
COWPER	William	RETIREMENT	117
COX	Marcelene	BABY/CHRISTENING	10
CRANE	Frank	FRIENDSHIP	60
CRASHAW	Richard	CHRISTMAS	35
CROWELL	Grace Noll	CHRISTMAS	42
CROWELL	Grace Noll	CHRISTMAS	32
CUMBERLAND	Bishop Richard	BIRTHDAY	24
CUMMINGS	E. E.	CONGRATULATIONS	45
CUMMINGS	Fr. Jerome	FRIENDSHIP	60
CUMMINS	Anna	FRIENDSHIP	60
CUOMO	Mario	FATHERS DAY	53
DACH	Simon	FRIENDSHIP	60
DALE	Evans	LEAVING/PARTING	80
D'ANGELO	Anthony J.	CONGRATULATIONS	46
DARWIN	Charles	FRIENDSHIP	60
DAVIS	Chili	BIRTHDAY	26
DAWSON	`Les	WEDDING	133
DAY	Doris	BIRTHDAY	31
DE CERVANTES	Miguel	FRIENDSHIP	59
DELILLE	Jacques	FRIENDSHIP	60
DENT	James	NEW HOME	106
DESBORDES-VALMORE	Marceline	WEDDING	131
DIANA	Princess of Wales	MOTHERS DAY	93
DICKENS	Charles	BABY/CHRISTENING	9
DICKENS	Charles	CHRISTMAS	34
DICKENS	Charles	CHRISTMAS	35
DICKENS	Charles	CHRISTMAS	36
DICKENS	Charles	CHRISTMAS	39
DICKENS	Charles	CHRISTMAS	39
DICKENS	Charles	CHRISTMAS	40
DICKINSON	Emily	LEAVING/PARTING	73
DILLER	Phyllis	BIRTHDAY	22
DILLER	Phyllis	RETIREMENT	114
DISRAELI	Benjamin	FRIENDSHIP	64
DISRAELI	Benjamin	THANKYOU	125
DODSLEY	Robert	LEAVING/PARTING	78
DODSLEY	Robert	LOVED ONE/VALENTINE	91
DOUBIAGO	Sharon	MOTHERS DAY	98
DRYDEN	John	LEAVING/PARTING	73
DRYDEN	John	LOVED ONE/VALENTINE	90
DUNCAN	Isadora	MOTHERS DAY	98
DUNNE	Finley Peter	GET WELL	67
DYER	Wayne	CONGRATULATIONS	44
DYKE	Henry Van	NEW HOME	105
EASON	Jim	BIRTHDAY	29
EBERS	George	FRIENDSHIP	60
ECKHART	Meister	THANKYOU	126
EDDISON	Thomas A.	PROMOTION	108
EDWARDS	Robert C.	FRIENDSHIP	60
EDWARDS	Tryon	LEAVING/PARTING	72
EDWARDS	Tryon	SORRY	122
ELIOT	George	FRIENDSHIP	60
ELIOTT	S.	BIRTHDAY	20
ELLEDGE	Scott	RETIREMENT	115
ELLIS	W. T.	CHRISTMAS	32
ELLIS	W. T.	CHRISTMAS	35
ELLIS	W. T.	CHRISTMAS	37
ELLIS	W. T.	CHRISTMAS	39
ELLISTON	George	THANKYOU	125
EMERSON	Ralph Waldo	CONGRATULATIONS	45
EMERSON	Ralph Waldo	FRIENDSHIP	62

EMERSON	Ralph Waldo	FRIENDSHIP	62
ESCHENBACH	Marie E.	LOVED ONE/VALENTINE	85
EVANS	Dale	RETIREMENT	118
EVANS	Dale	LEAVING/PARTING	80
FARR	Hilda Brett	FRIENDSHIP	62
FEATHER	William	MOTHERS DAY	94
FELT-BARDON	Martha	RETIREMENT	120
FIELDS	Wayne	GET WELL	67
FORBES	Malcolm	PROMOTION	109
FORBES	Malcolm	RETIREMENT	115
FORBES	Malcolm	RETIREMENT	115
FORBES	Malcolm	RETIREMENT	120
FORD	Henry	BIRTHDAY	20
FOREMAN	George	RETIREMENT	112
FORSTER	E. M.	CHRISTMAS	39
FOSDICK	Harry Emerson	RETIREMENT	112
FOSDICK	Harry Emerson	RETIREMENT	119
FOX	Jim	CONGRATULATIONS	45
FOX	Jim	GOING TO UNIVERSITY/COLLEGE	70
FRANKEN	Rose	LOVED ONE/VALENTINE	87
FRANKLIN	Benjamin	BIRTHDAY	20
FRANKLIN	Benjamin	CONGRATULATIONS	44
FRANKLIN	J.	LOVED ONE/VALENTINE	88
FREUD	Sigmund	FATHERS DAY	51
FRIEDMANN	Isaac	SORRY	122
FROMM	Erich	LOVED ONE/VALENTINE	85
FROMM	Erich	MOTHERS DAY	98
FROST	Robert	BIRTHDAY	19
FROST	Robert	FATHERS DAY	53
FROST	Robert	LOVED ONE/VALENTINE	88
FROST	Robert	WEDDING	133
FUCHS	Joanna	THANKYOU	130
FUCHS	Karl	THANKYOU	129
GALBRAITH	J. K.	DIVORCE	48
GANDHI	Mohandas K.	LOVED ONE/VALENTINE	83
GARLAND	Judy	ANNIVERSARY	4
GARLAND	Judy	LOVED ONE/VALENTINE	87
GARNER	Cindy	DIVORCE	51
GARRETTY	Marion C.	MOTHERS DAY	96
GAY	John	LEAVING/PARTING	75
GAY	John	RETIREMENT	117
GAY	John	RETIREMENT	117
GEDDES	Anne	FATHERS DAY	53
GEISEL	Theodor Seuss	LOVED ONE/VALENTINE	92
GELBART	Larry	DIVORCE	49
GENEEN	Harold	PROMOTION	108
GHANDI	Claudia	LEAVING/PARTING	77
GHANDI	Claudia	LOVED ONE/VALENTINE	90
GIBRAN	Kahil	BEREAVEMENT/SYMPATHY	15
GIBRAN	Kahlil	FRIENDSHIP	61
GIBRAN	Kahlil	LOVED ONE/VALENTINE	84
GIBRAN	Kahlil	LOVED ONE/VALENTINE	84
GIBRAN	Kahlil	LOVED ONE/VALENTINE	84
GIBRAN	Kahlil	LOVED ONE/VALENTINE	90
GLASER	Sherry	BABY/CHRISTENING	12
GLENCONNE	Pamela	BABY/CHRISTENING	9
GLENCONNE	Pamela	MOTHERS DAY	103
GLENN	John	BIRTHDAY	22
GLENN	John	BIRTHDAY	23
GOGH	Vincent van	ANNIVERSARY	5
GOLDSMITH	Oliver	LEAVING/PARTING	78
GOLDSMITH	Oliver	RETIREMENT	111

GOTTESMAN	David M.	FATHERS DAY	53
GREER	Germaine	WEDDING	131
GRENON	R. M.	LEAVING/PARTING	78
GRENON	R. M.	LOVED ONE/VALENTINE	91
GRIER	John P.	BIRTHDAY	23
GRIMUTTER	Leslie	GET WELL	68
GROUCHO	Marx	RETIREMENT	115
GROUCHO	Marx	RETIREMENT	116
GROUCHO	Marx	WEDDING	136
HALEN	Halen	LOVED ONE/VALENTINE	85
HALLIBURTON	Richard	CONGRATULATIONS	45
HALM	Friedrich	WEDDING	132
HAMPTON	Lionel	THANKYOU	129
HARMON	Graycie	MOTHERS DAY	96
HARRIS	Ella	RETIREMENT	110
HARRIS	Ella	RETIREMENT	116
HAWKINS	Maureen	MOTHERS DAY	103
HAYES	Helen	LOVED ONE/VALENTINE	82
HAYNES	Margie	BABY/CHRISTENING	11
HEARN	Barry	PROMOTION	108
HEINLEIN	Robert A.	LOVED ONE/VALENTINE	84
HEIST	Dan	SORRY	121
HEMANS	Felicia	CHRISTMAS	40
HEMINGWAY	Ernest	RETIREMENT	114
HERBERT	George	FATHERS DAY	53
HERBERT	George	FRIENDSHIP	62
HERBERT	George	MOTHERS DAY	98
HERROLD	Don	BABY/CHRISTENING	11
HESS	John D.	PROMOTION	109
HESSE	Herman	ANNIVERSARY	5
HILL	Benny	CHRISTMAS	36
HILLIS	Burton	CHRISTMAS	37
HILLIS	Burton	CHRISTMAS	41
HOLLAND	Canon Scott	BEREAVEMENT/SYMPATHY	15
HOLMES	Oliver Wendell	LOVED ONE/VALENTINE	89
HOLMES	Oliver Wendell	MOTHERS DAY	93
HOLMES	Oliver Wendell	MOTHERS DAY	99
HOLMES	Oliver Wendell	NEW HOME	105
HOLMES	John Andrew	BIRTHDAY	23
HOLMES	Marjorie	CHRISTMAS	39
HOMER	Homer	WEDDING	132
HOPE	Bob	BIRTHDAY	19
HOPE	Bob	BIRTHDAY	29
HOPE	Bob	BIRTHDAY	30
HOPPER	Grace	SORRY	122
HOPPER	Grace	SORRY	123
HORACE	Horace	GOING TO UNIVERSITY/COLLEGE	70
HORACE	Horace	WEDDING	131
HOUSMAN	Lawrence	BABY/CHRISTENING	12
HOWE	Ed	BABY/CHRISTENING	10
HOWE	Ed	BABY/CHRISTENING	14
HUBBARD	Elbert	GOING TO UNIVERSITY/COLLEGE	70
HUBBARD	Frank McKinney	NEW HOME	106
HUBBARD	Ken	BABY/CHRISTENING	11
HUBBARD	Kin	CHRISTMAS	40
HUBBARD	Kin	CHRISTMAS	40
HUGO	Victor	ANNIVERSARY	5
HUGO	Victor	MOTHERS DAY	97
HUMPHREY	Hubert	GET WELL	67
HURSTON	Zora Neale	LOVED ONE/VALENTINE	89
IRONS	Jeremy	LOVED ONE/VALENTINE	88
JARVIS	Anna	MOTHERS DAY	104

JAYDE	Jayde	LEAVING/PARTING	74
JEROME	Saint	FRIENDSHIP	62
JERROLD	Douglas	WEDDING	131
JOHNSON	Kimberly	SORRY	122
JOHNSON	Philander Chase	BIRTHDAY	19
JOHNSON	Philander Chase	RETIREMENT	110
JOHNSON	Samuel	FATHERS DAY	52
JOHNSON	Lynn	SORRY	121
JONES	Franklin P.	BABY/CHRISTENING	10
JONES	Franklin P.	LOVED ONE/VALENTINE	83
JONES	Sir John Harvey	PROMOTION	108
JONG	Erica	LEAVING/PARTING	80
JONG	Erica	WEDDING	134
JONSON	Ben	LEAVING/PARTING	73
JONSON	Ben	RETIREMENT	118
JORDAN	Tenneva	MOTHERS DAY	94
JOUBERT	Joseph	FATHERS DAY	52
JOYCE	James	MOTHERS DAY	93
JOYCE	James	MOTHERS DAY	100
JULE	Hartman	RETIREMENT	111
JULE	Hartman	RETIREMENT	112
KAFKA	Franz	BIRTHDAY	26
KATZ	Ellie	GET WELL	67
KEANE	Molly	BIRTHDAY	24
KEATS	John	LOVED ONE/VALENTINE	83
KEEN	Sam	LOVED ONE/VALENTINE	84
KEEN	Sam	WEDDING	135
KEILLOR	Garrison	FATHERS DAY	53
KEILLOR	Garrison	RETIREMENT	118
KELLAND	Clarence Budington	FATHERS DAY	53
KELLER	Helen	FRIENDSHIP	63
KEMBLE	Frances Anne	LEAVING/PARTING	74
KENNEDY	John F.	THANKYOU	126
KERR	Jean	WEDDING	132
KEYNES	John Maynard	GOING TO UNIVERSITY/COLLEGE	71
KIMBROUGH	Emily	SORRY	123
KINGMA	Daphne Rose	THANKYOU	128
KIPLING	Rudyard	MOTHERS DAY	100
KNUDSEN	Kay	LEAVING/PARTING	73
KNUDSEN	Kay	LEAVING/PARTING	76
KOCH	Edward	CONGRATULATIONS	45
LAMB	Charles	MOTHERS DAY	99
LARCOM	Lucy	BIRTHDAY	25
LARDNER	Ring	LOVED ONE/VALENTINE	85
LARSON	Doug	NEW HOME	106
LARSON	Doug	RETIREMENT	111
LATET	Carrie	MOTHERS DAY	100
LATET	Carrie	MOTHERS DAY	102
LAUDER	Sir Harry	LOVED ONE/VALENTINE	86
LAURENCE	Dr. Peter J.	LEAVING/PARTING	80
LAURENCE	Dr. Peter J.	PROMOTION	109
LAURENCE	Margaret	SORRY	122
LEMONS	Abe	RETIREMENT	110
LENIN	Nikolai	GET WELL	68
LENNON	John	FRIENDSHIP	64
LENNON	John	WEDDING	133
LENO	Jay	CHRISTMAS	42
LESCHEN	Caryn	BIRTHDAY	27
LEUNIG	Michael	ANNIVERSARY	7
LEVINE	Stephen	SORRY	123
LEWIS	Jerry	FATHERS DAY	54
LIEBMAN	Joshua	LOVED ONE/VALENTINE	85

LINCOLN	Abraham	BIRTHDAY	23
LINCOLN	Abraham	LEAVING/PARTING	81
LINCOLN	Abraham	MOTHERS DAY	94
LINCOLN	Abraham	MOTHERS DAY	100
LONDON	Jack	LEAVING/PARTING	81
LONGFELLOW	Henry Wadsworth	RETIREMENT	110
LONGFELLOW	Henry Wadsworth	BIRTHDAY	20
LONGFELLOW	Henry Wadsworth	CHRISTMAS	34
LONGFELLOW	Henry Wadsworth	CHRISTMAS	38
LOREN	Sophia	MOTHERS DAY	95
LORENZONI	Larry	BIRTHDAY	19
LORIMER	George	GOING TO UNIVERSITY/COLLEGE	71
LOWELL	Amy	LEAVING/PARTING	74
LOWELL	James Russell	MOTHERS DAY	97
LOWELL	James Russell	THANKYOU	124
LUBBOCK	J.	RETIREMENT	111
LUDWIG VAN	Beethoven	FRIENDSHIP	63
LUTHER	Martin	WEDDING	132
LUTHER KING JR	Martin	FRIENDSHIP	63
LYTE	Henry Francis	BEREAVEMENT/SYMPATHY	16
MABI	Hamilton Wright	CHRISTMAS	36
MABIE	Hamilton Wright	CHRISTMAS	38
MAHTAR	Harry	RETIREMENT	113
MAISONROUGE	Jacques	PROMOTION	109
MANVILLE	Tommy	DIVORCE	48
MARGOLIUS	Hans	LOVED ONE/VALENTINE	85
MARQUEZ	Gabriel Garcia	FATHERS DAY	55
MARQUIS	Don	BIRTHDAY	27
MARSTON	Ralph	THANKYOU	126
MARSTON	Ralph	THANKYOU	127
MARTIN	Dean	RETIREMENT	114
MASSIEU	Jean Baptiste	THANKYOU	125
MAUR	Francois	LOVED ONE/VALENTINE	85
MAXWELL	Florida Scott	MOTHERS DAY	93
MAYOR	John	FATHERS DAY	51
MC CULLOUGH	Colleen	BIRTHDAY	25
MC GINLEY	Phyllis	FATHERS DAY	52
MC GINLEY	Phyllis	MOTHERS DAY	101
MC GORTY	Danny	RETIREMENT	116
MC GREW	Steve	DIVORCE	48
MC INTYRE	Andy	GOING TO UNIVERSITY/COLLEGE	71
MC KAY	David O.	THANKYOU	127
MC LAUGHLIN	Mignon	ANNIVERSARY	3
MC LAUGHLIN	Mignon	LOVED ONE/VALENTINE	89
MC LAUGHLIN	Mignon	SORRY	122
MCOMBER	Susan	BABY/CHRISTENING	11
MEIR	Golda	MOTHERS DAY	95
MENCK	H. L.	LOVED ONE/VALENTINE	84
MERWIN	WS	LEAVING/PARTING	75
MICHELS JR.	James P.	FRIENDSHIP	65
MIDLER	Bette	BIRTHDAY	28
MILLAY	Edna St. Vincent	LEAVING/PARTING	74
MILLER	Dennis	CHRISTMAS	36
MILLER	Harlan	CHRISTMAS	39
MILLER	Susan	RETIREMENT	119
MILNE	A. A.	LEAVING/PARTING	76
MILNE	A. A.	LOVED ONE/VALENTINE	90
MILNE	A. A.	RETIREMENT	113
MOLIERE	Moliere	LOVED ONE/VALENTINE	82
MONKHOUSE	Bob	RETIREMENT	116
MONROE	D. D.	CHRISTMAS	40
MONTGOMERY	Robert	NEW HOME	105

MOORE	George	LOVED ONE/VALENTINE	89
MOORE	Thomas	LOVED ONE/VALENTINE	83
MOORE	Thomas	WEDDING	131
MORLEY	Christopher	NEW HOME	106
MORRISON	Toni	MOTHERS DAY	97
MOTHER TERESA	Mother Teresa	FRIENDSHIP	62
MOTHER TERESA	Mother Teresa	LOVED ONE/VALENTINE	83
MOTHER TERESA	Mother Teresa	LOVED ONE/VALENTINE	89
MOTHER TERESA	Mother Teresa	LOVED ONE/VALENTINE	89
MOYERS	Bill	WEDDING	131
MULOCK	Dinah Maria	ANNIVERSARY	6
MURRAY	Patrick	WEDDING	133
NASH	Ogden	BIRTHDAY	22
NASH	Ogden	BIRTHDAY	24
NASH	Ogden	WEDDING	132
NAYLOR	Gloria	FATHERS DAY	51
NECKER	Suzanne	LOVED ONE/VALENTINE	85
NELSON	Carol	CHRISTMAS	38
NELSON	Willie	DIVORCE	49
NICHOLS	Beverly	WEDDING	131
NIETZSCHE	Nietzsche	BEREAVEMENT/SYMPATHY	15
O'MALLEY	Austin	FATHERS DAY	55
ORBEN	Robert	BABY/CHRISTENING	10
ORISON	Swett Marden	GET WELL	67
O'ROURKE	P. J.	CHRISTMAS	38
O'ROURKE	P. J.	CHRISTMAS	42
ORWELL	George	BIRTHDAY	29
OSGOOD	Charles	BABY/CHRISTENING	9
PAGELS	Douglas	RETIREMENT	113
PALAHNIUK	Chuck	ANNIVERSARY	5
PARSONS	Elia	BABY/CHRISTENING	11
PAUL	Robert	BABY/CHRISTENING	9
PEALE	Norman Vincent	CHRISTMAS	35
PEALE	Norman Vincent	CHRISTMAS	36
PEALE	Norman Vincent	CHRISTMAS	38
PENCOVICI	Arie	CONGRATULATIONS	44
PENNEY	J. C.	PROMOTION	108
PERELMAN	S. J.	ANNIVERSARY	8
PERRET	Gene	ANNIVERSARY	6
PERRET	Gene	RETIREMENT	110
PERRET	Gene	RETIREMENT	111
PERRET	Gene	RETIREMENT	112
PERRET	Gene	RETIREMENT	112
PERRET	Gene	RETIREMENT	112
PERRET	Gene	RETIREMENT	113
PERRET	Gene	RETIREMENT	114
PERRET	Gene	RETIREMENT	115
PERRET	Gene	RETIREMENT	116
PERRET	Gene	RETIREMENT	116
PERRET	Gene	RETIREMENT	119
PESANTE	Zoraida	MOTHERS DAY	102
PETTY	Tom	LEAVING/PARTING	76
PETTY	Tom	LEAVING/PARTING	80
PETTY	Tom	RETIREMENT	118
PHARO	Agnes M.	CHRISTMAS	42
PHARO	Agnes M.	CHRISTMAS	32
PHARO	Agnes M.	CHRISTMAS	37
PHILIPS	Emo	GOING TO UNIVERSITY/COLLEGE	71
PICASSO	Pablo	LOVED ONE/VALENTINE	89
PICASSO	Pablo	BIRTHDAY	20
PIKE	Albert	THANKYOU	128
PITKIN	W. B.	BIRTHDAY	24

PITTMAN	Frank	ANNIVERSARY	6
PIZER	Marjorie	BEREAVEMENT/SYMPATHY	16
PLATH	Sylvia	RETIREMENT	113
PLATO	Plato	LOVED ONE/VALENTINE	83
PLAUTUS	Plautus	BIRTHDAY	23
POE	Edgar Allan	MOTHERS DAY	101
POLSON	Bronwyn	FRIENDSHIP	64
POPE	Alexander	LOVED ONE/VALENTINE	91
POWELL	Anthony	BIRTHDAY	23
PROCHNOW	H. V.	BIRTHDAY	25
PUBLILIUS	Syrus	FATHERS DAY	54
PULSIFER	Catherine	ANNIVERSARY	5
PULSIFER	Catherine	ANNIVERSARY	6
RADICI	Adabella	MOTHERS DAY	96
RADICI	Adabella	MOTHERS DAY	98
RADNER	Gilda	LEAVING/PARTING	78
RADNER	Gilda	LOVED ONE/VALENTINE	91
RAJNEESH	Rajneesh	BABY/CHRISTENING	14
RAJNEESH	Rajneesh	MOTHERS DAY	94
REID	Libby	BIRTHDAY	28
RENKEL	Ruth E.	FATHERS DAY	54
RENKEL	Ruth E.	MOTHERS DAY	104
RENOIR	Jean	BIRTHDAY	25
RICE	Helen Steiner	CHRISTMAS	37
RICE	Helen Steiner	CHRISTMAS	41
RICHTER	Jean Paul	RETIREMENT	117
RICHTER	Johann Paul Friedrich	GET WELL	67
RICKEY	Branch	RETIREMENT	114
RICKEY	Branch Rickey	BIRTHDAY	30
RILKE	Rainer Maria	WEDDING	131
RIVERS	Joan	BIRTHDAY	29
ROBINSON	Edwin Arlington	THANKYOU	128
ROCHEFOUCAULD (Duc de la)	Francois	LEAVING/PARTING	79
ROCHEFOUCAULD (Duc de la)	Francois	RETIREMENT	120
RODDICK	Anita	PROMOTION	108
RODDICK	Anita	PROMOTION	108
RODRIGUEZ	Chi Chi	RETIREMENT	110
ROGERS	Dale Evans	CHRISTMAS	42
ROGERS	Will	RETIREMENT	112
ROGERS	Will	RETIREMENT	115
RONAN	Bill	MOTHERS DAY	104
ROONEY	Andy	CHRISTMAS	35
ROSSETTI	Christina	CHRISTMAS	37
ROWE	Nicholas	LEAVING/PARTING	74
ROWLAND	Helen	BIRTHDAY	28
ROWLAND	Helen	DIVORCE	49
ROWLAND	Helen	FATHERS DAY	55
ROWLAND	Helen	LEAVING/PARTING	77
ROWLAND	Helen	WEDDING	136
RUDNER	Rita	WEDDING	131
RUNDEL	Augusta E.	CHRISTMAS	43
RUTHIE	Ruthie	LEAVING/PARTING	74
RYAN	Joe	NEW HOME	106
SABOL	Blair	BIRTHDAY	25
SAINT-EXUPERY	Antoine de	ANNIVERSARY	3
SAKI	Saki	LOVED ONE/VALENTINE	86
SARTON	May	NEW HOME	106
SCHNEERSON	Menachem Mendel	BIRTHDAY	26
SCHOPENHAUER	Arthur	BIRTHDAY	28
SCHULER	Loring A.	CHRISTMAS	39
SCHWEITZER	Albert	THANKYOU	127
SCOTT	Sir Walter	CHRISTMAS	36

SEARS	J. P.	BIRTHDAY	23
SECUNDA	Victoria	MOTHERS DAY	99
SEIFERT	Barbara Christine	BABY/CHRISTENING	13
SENECA	Seneca	THANKYOU	129
SEUSS	Dr.	BIRTHDAY	21
SEUSS	Dr.	CHRISTMAS	33
SEUSS	Dr.	CONGRATULATIONS	47
SEUSS	Dr.	LEAVING/PARTING	79
SHAKESPEARE	William	BIRTHDAY	30
SHAKESPEARE	William	LEAVING/PARTING	76
SHAKESPEARE	William	LOVED ONE/VALENTINE	82
SHAKESPEARE	William	MOTHERS DAY	95
SHAKESPEARE	William	RETIREMENT	118
SHAKESPEARE	William	THANKYOU	124
SHAKESPEARE	William	THANKYOU	125
SHAKESPEARE	William	THANKYOU	125
SHAKESPEARE	William	WEDDING	132
SHAW	George Bernard	BIRTHDAY	28
SHAW	George Bernard	GET WELL	66
SHAW	George Bernard	WEDDING	136
SHEEHY	Gail	RETIREMENT	112
SHERRIFF	R. C.	RETIREMENT	110
SIGNORET	Simone	ANNIVERSARY	4
SMITH	Doris	BABY/CHRISTENING	9
SMITH	Elinor Goulding	BABY/CHRISTENING	10
SMITH	Hannah W.	BABY/CHRISTENING	12
SMITH	Hannah W.	MOTHERS DAY	104
SMITH	Roy L.	CHRISTMAS	35
SMITH	Sydney	LOVED ONE/VALENTINE	82
SOCKMAN	Ralph W.	ANNIVERSARY	4
SONI	M. K.	RETIREMENT	113
SONI	M. K.	RETIREMENT	115
SOUTHARD	John E.	THANKYOU	124
SOUTHEY	Robert	BIRTHDAY	30
SOUTHEY	Robert	RETIREMENT	118
SPARKS	Nicholas	LEAVING/PARTING	76
SPOCKS	Benjamin	MOTHERS DAY	103
STAPLETON	Ruth Carter	CHRISTMAS	33
STEIN	Gertrude	BIRTHDAY	20
STERN	G. B.	THANKYOU	124
STEVENSON	Robert Louis	CONGRATULATIONS	44
STEVENSON	Robert Louis	FRIENDSHIP	64
STONE	Elizabeth	BABY/CHRISTENING	9
STOPPARD	Tom	BIRTHDAY	23
STOWE	Harriet Beecher	BABY/CHRISTENING	11
STOWE	Harriet Beecher	BEREAVEMENT/SYMPATHY	17
STREEP	Meryl	MOTHERS DAY	96
STRINDBERG	August	FATHERS DAY	54
STRINDBERG	August	FATHERS DAY	51
SUNDAY	Billy	LOVED ONE/VALENTINE	85
SUNDE	Karen	ANNIVERSARY	7
SVIGN	Mariede	FRIENDSHIP	64
SWEAT	Keith	ANNIVERSARY	7
SWEENEY	Paul	ANNIVERSARY	3
SWIFT	Jonathan	BIRTHDAY	23
SWIFT	Jonathan	BIRTHDAY	26
SWINBURNE	Algernon Charles	BABY/CHRISTENING	9
TABRON	Carole	BABY/CHRISTENING	13
TALMAGE	T. Dewitt	MOTHERS DAY	98
TAYLOR	Ann	MOTHERS DAY	98
TAYLOR	Anne	MOTHERS DAY	98
TEILHARD (DE CHARDIN)	Pierre	FRIENDSHIP	60

TENNYSON	Alfred	LEAVING/PARTING	75
THACKERAY	William Makepeace	MOTHERS DAY	98
THOMAS	David	THANKYOU	124
THOMPSON	Dorothy	BIRTHDAY	23
THOMPSON	Francis	LOVED ONE/VALENTINE	91
THOREAU	Henry David	CONGRATULATIONS	44
THOREAU	Henry David	BABY/CHRISTENING	13
THOREAU	Henry David	FRIENDSHIP	63
THOREAU	Henry David	GET WELL	66
THOREAU	Henry David	LEAVING/PARTING	73
THOREAU	Henry David	RETIREMENT	117
TRACY	Brian	CONGRATULATIONS	44
TRUMAN	Harry	MOTHERS DAY	101
TRUMAN	Margaret	FATHERS DAY	54
TUCKER	Sophie	BIRTHDAY	24
TURNER	Lana	WEDDING	133
TUSSER	Thomas	CHRISTMAS	35
TUSSER	Thomas	CHRISTMAS	37
TWAIN	Mark	ANNIVERSARY	5
TWAIN	Mark	BABY/CHRISTENING	11
TWAIN	Mark	BABY/CHRISTENING	13
TWAIN	Mark	BIRTHDAY	29
TWAIN	Mark	GET WELL	66
TWAIN	Mark	MOTHERS DAY	100
TWAIN	Mark	THANKYOU	125
VALVANO	Jim	FATHERS DAY	51
VAN AMBURGH	Fred de Witt	THANKYOU	128
VAN MUNCH BELLING	Franz Joseph	LOVED ONE/VALENTINE	82
VARDON	Harry	RETIREMENT	112
VAUGHN	Bill	GOING TO UNIVERSITY/COLLEGE	70
VERMONT	Mildred B.	MOTHERS DAY	93
VIORST	Judith	LOVED ONE/VALENTINE	85
VOLTAIRE	Voltaire	BIRTHDAY	28
VOLTAIRE	Voltaire	GET WELL	67
VOLTAIRE	Voltaire	THANKYOU	129
VON GOETHE	Johann	LOVED ONE/VALENTINE	82
VON GOETHE	Johann Wolfgang	WEDDING	132
VRIES	Peter de	MOTHERS DAY	94
VRIES	Peter de	ANNIVERSARY	6
WADSWORTH	Charles	FATHERS DAY	54
WAGNER	Jane	BIRTHDAY	29
WALPOLE	Sr. Hugh	ANNIVERSARY	6
WARD	William Arthur	CONGRATULATIONS	45
WARD	William Arthur	THANKYOU	126
WARD	William Arthur	THANKYOU	126
WARNER	Charles Dudley	NEW HOME	105
WASSERSTEIN	Wendy	CONGRATULATIONS	44
WATTERSON	Bill	RETIREMENT	112
WATTS	Gordon T.	THANKYOU	126
WEEDON	Flavia	LEAVING/PARTING	80
WEEMS	Renita	MOTHERS DAY	99
WEILACHER	G. M.	NEW HOME	106
WELLS	Carolyn	CHRISTMAS	39
WENG	Chu Hui	GET WELL	69
WESTWOOD	Anna	LOVED ONE/VALENTINE	90
WHIPP	Deborah	CHRISTMAS	38
WHITTIER	John Greenleaf	CHRISTMAS	41
WIESEL	Elie	THANKYOU	129
WIGGIN	Kate Douglas	MOTHERS DAY	99
WILCOX	Ella Wheeler	SORRY	122
WILDE	Larry	CHRISTMAS	40
WILDE	Oscar	BIRTHDAY	19

WILDE	Oscar	BIRTHDAY	28
WILDE	Oscar	GOING TO UNIVERSITY/COLLEGE	70
WILDE	Oscar	MOTHERS DAY	95
WILDE	Oscar	SORRY	123
WILDE	Oscar	THANKYOU	125
WILDE	Oscar	WEDDING	134
WILDER	Laura Ingalls	CHRISTMAS	34
WILDER	Thornton	THANKYOU	125
WILKINSON	Lee	FRIENDSHIP	63
WILLIAMS	Pearl	GET WELL	68
WILLIAMS	Robin	DIVORCE	48
WILLIS	Nathaniel Parker	MOTHERS DAY	101
WILLSON	Meredith	LEAVING/PARTING	76
WILMOT	John	BABY/CHRISTENING	10
WILSON	Flip	GET WELL	66
WILSON	Tom	BIRTHDAY	30
WILSON	Woodrow	FRIENDSHIP	62
WINFREY	Oprah	BIRTHDAY	25
WINFREY	Oprah	MOTHERS DAY	102
WINTERS	Wayne F.	MOTHERS DAY	102
WODEHOUSE	P. G.	SORRY	121
WOOLF	Virginia	BIRTHDAY	26
WORDSWORTH	William	RETIREMENT	114
WRIGHT	Stephen	BIRTHDAY	29
YOUNG	Edward	LEAVING/PARTING	76
YOUNGMAN	Henny	LOVED ONE/VALENTINE	83
YOUNGMAN	Henry	WEDDING	136
YUTANG	Lin	MOTHERS DAY	103
ZSA ZSA GABOR	Zsa Zsa Gabor	LOVED ONE/VALENTINE	82